POSSESSIONS™

BOOK THREE

THE BETTER HOUSE TRAP

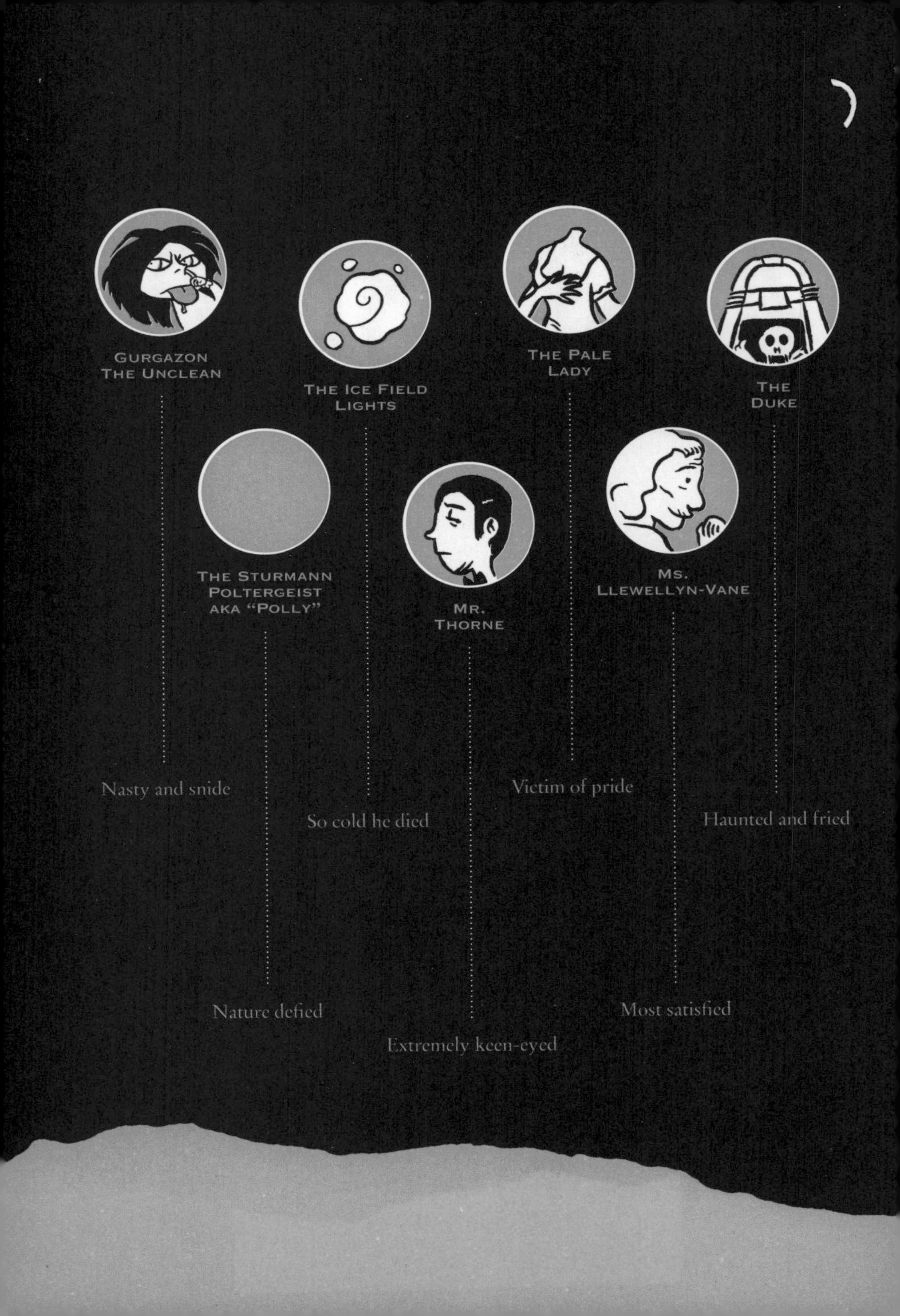

Gurgazon The Unclean
Nasty and snide
The Ice Field Lights
So cold he died
The Pale Lady
Victim of pride
The Duke
Haunted and fried
The Sturmann Poltergeist aka "Polly"
Nature defied
Mr. Thorne
Extremely keen-eyed
Ms. Llewellyn-Vane
Most satisfied

POSSESSIONS

BOOK THREE
THE BETTER HOUSE TRAP

WRITTEN & ILLUSTRATED BY
RAY FAWKES

DESIGN BY
KEITH WOOD

EDITED BY
JILL BEATON

Oni Press, Inc.

PUBLISHER **Joe Nozemack**

EDITOR IN CHIEF **James Lucas Jones**

MARKETING DIRECTOR **Cory Casoni**

ART DIRECTOR **Keith Wood**

OPERATIONS DIRECTOR **George Rohac**

EDITOR **Jill Beaton**

EDITOR **Charlie Chu**

DIGITAL PREPRESS LEAD **Troy Look**

Possessions, Volume 3, February 2012. Published by Oni Press, Inc.
1305 SE Martin Luther King Jr. Blvd., Suite A, Portland, OR 97214.
Possessions is ™ & © 2012 Ray Fawkes and Piper Snow Productions, Ltd.
All rights reserved. Unless otherwise specified, all other material © 2012
Oni Press, Inc. Oni Press logo and icon are ™ & © 2012 Oni Press, Inc.
All rights reserved. Oni Press logo and icon artwork created by
Dave Gibbons. The events, institutions, and characters presented
in this book are fictional. Any resemblance to actual persons,
living or dead, is purely coincidental. No portion of this
publication may be reproduced, by any means, without the
express written permission of the copyright holders.

Oni Press Inc.
1305 SE Martin Luther King Jr. Blvd.
Suite A
Portland, OR 97214

WWW.ONIPRESS.COM

First Edition: February 2012

ISBN 978-1-934964-76-7
Library of Congress Control Number: 2011911369

1 3 5 7 9 10 8 6 4 2

PRINTED IN CANADA

AND THIS ONE'S FOR HOHO.

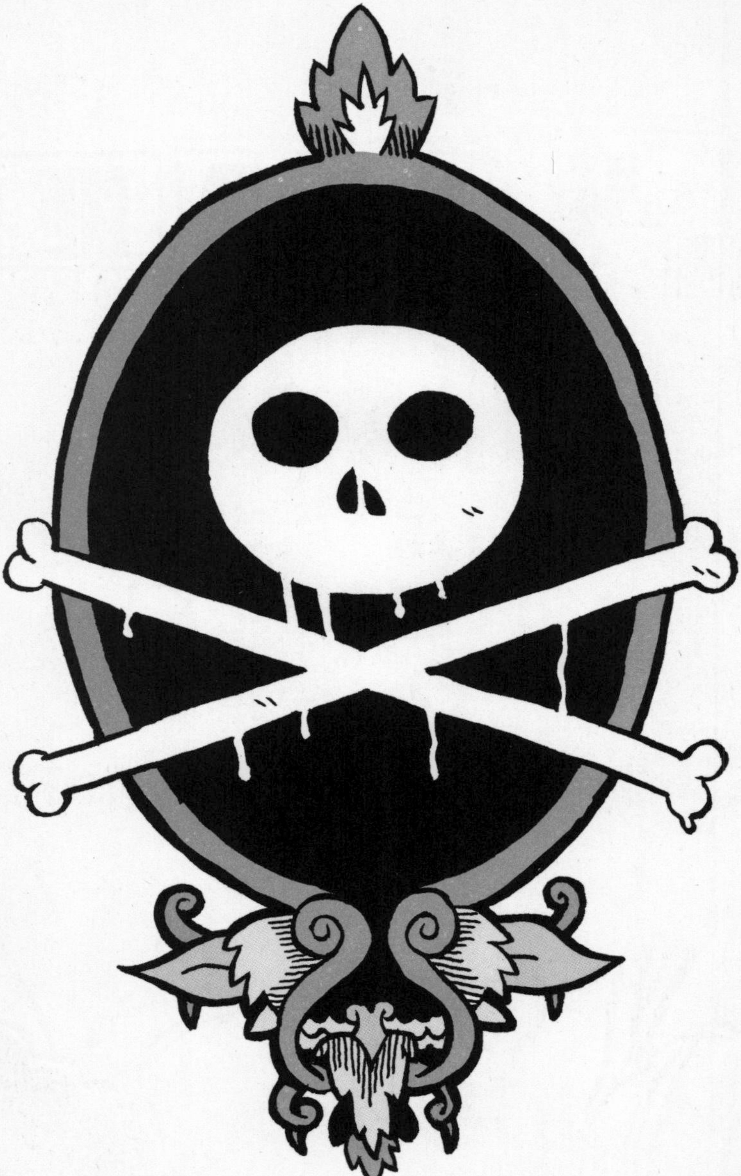

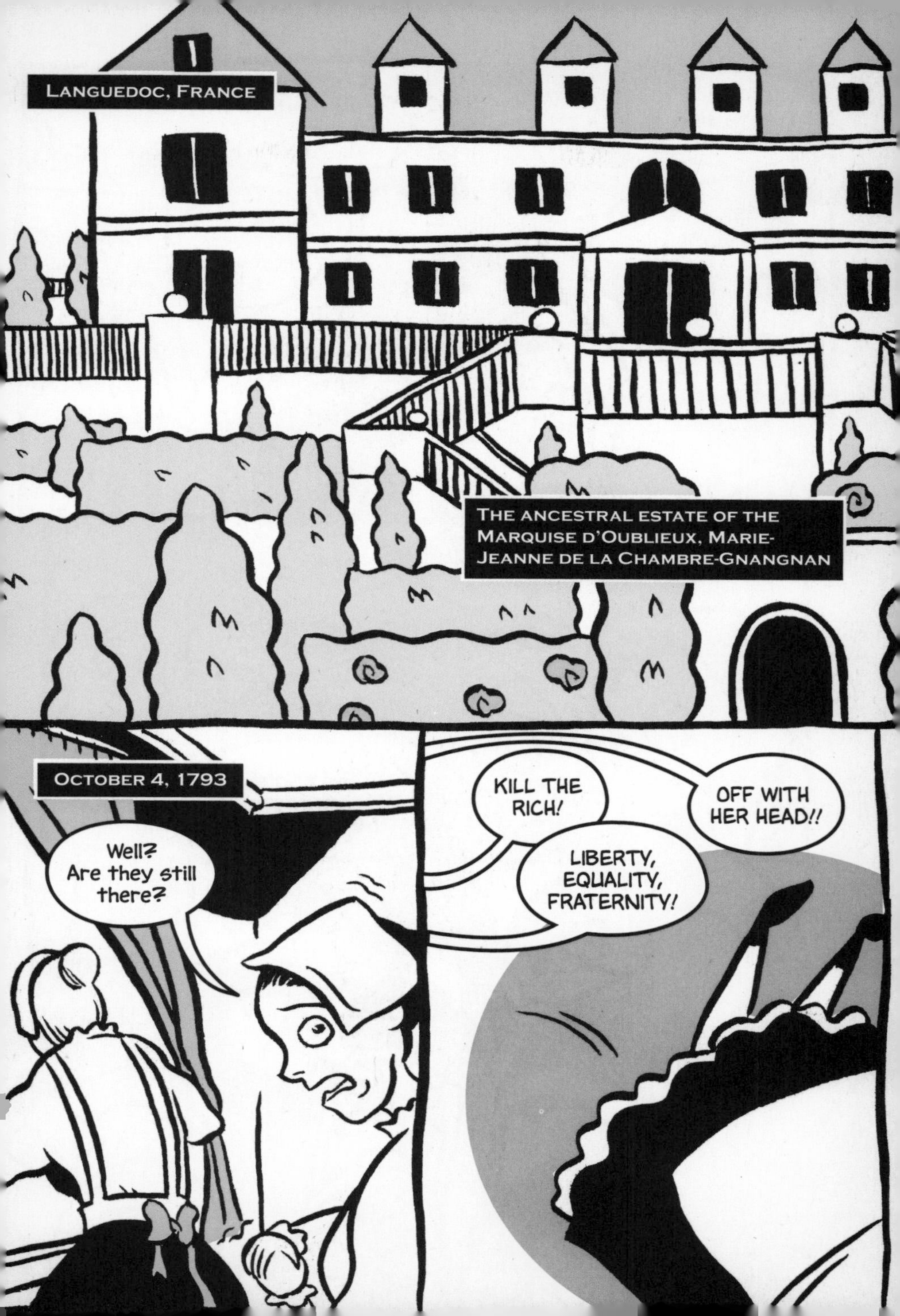
Languedoc, France
The ancestral estate of the Marquise d'Oublieux, Marie-Jeanne de la Chambre-Gnangnan
October 4, 1793
Well? Are they still there?
Kill the rich!
Off with her head!!
Liberty, equality, fraternity!

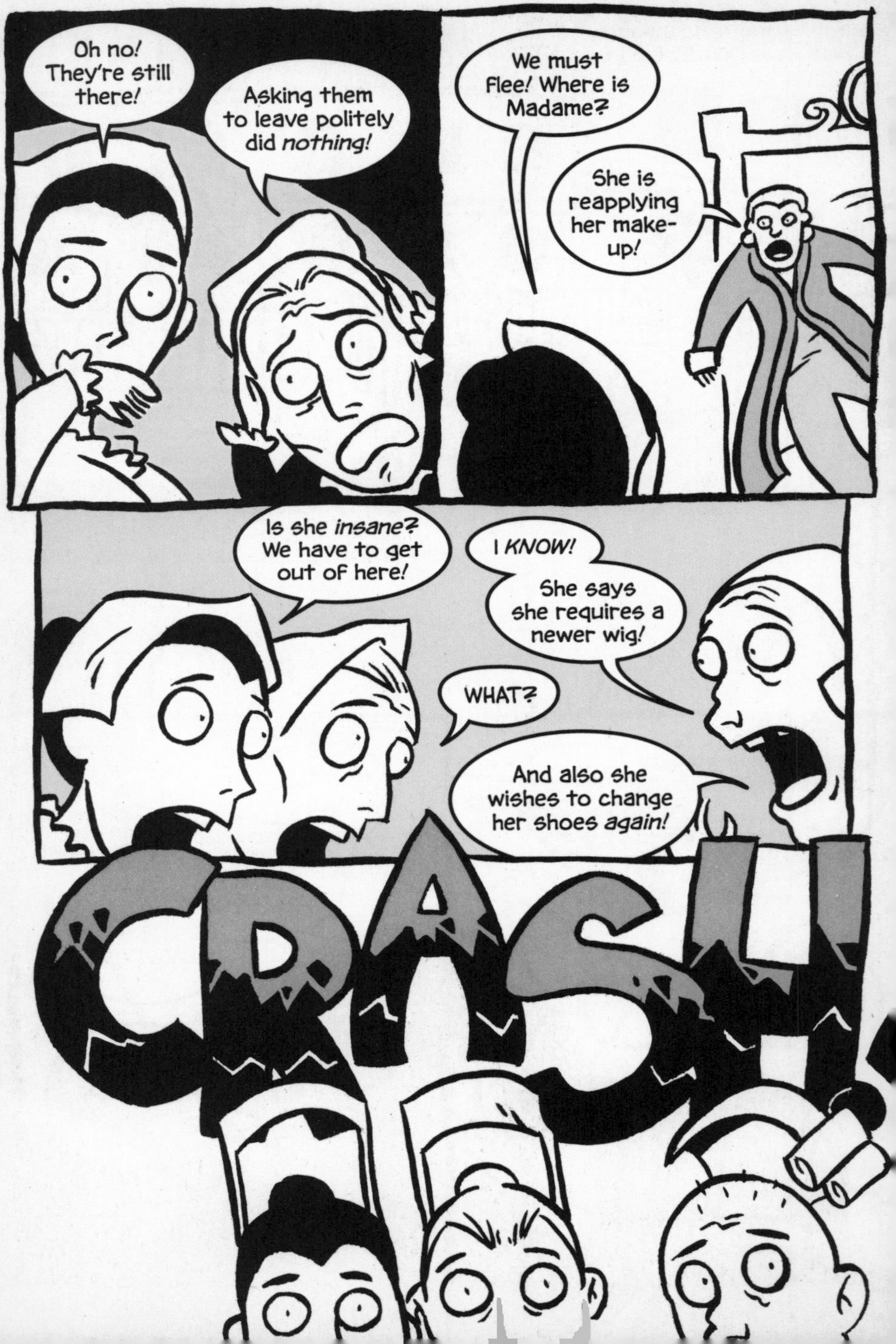
Oh no! They're still there!
Asking them to leave politely did *nothing*!
We must flee! Where is Madame?
She is reapplying her make-up!
Is she *insane*? We have to get out of here!
I *KNOW*!
She says she requires a newer wig!
WHAT?
And also she wishes to change her shoes *again*!
CRASH!

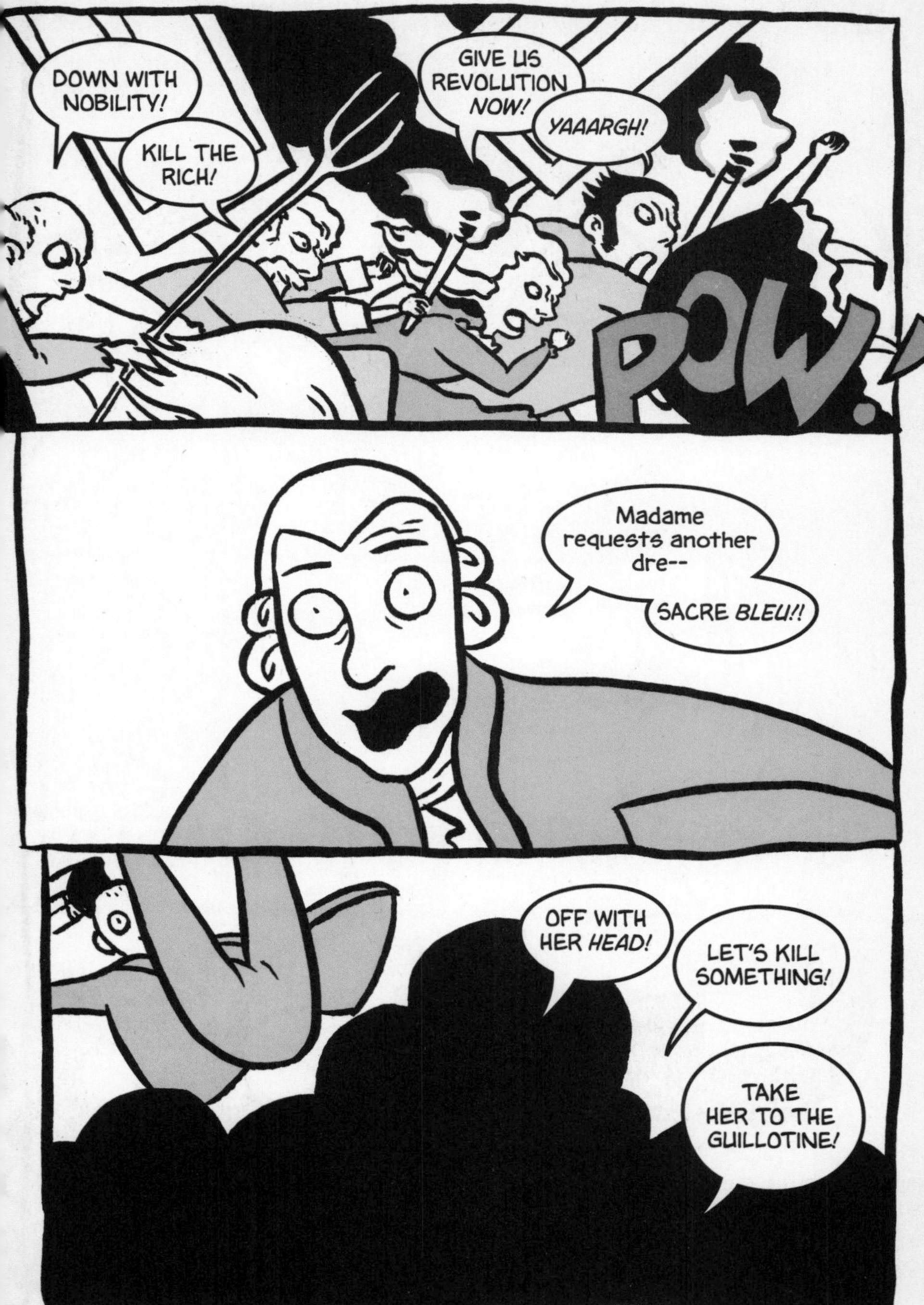
DOWN WITH NOBILITY!
KILL THE RICH!
GIVE US REVOLUTION NOW!
YAAARGH!
POW!
Madame requests another dre--
SACRE BLEU!!
OFF WITH HER HEAD!
LET'S KILL SOMETHING!
TAKE HER TO THE GUILLOTINE!

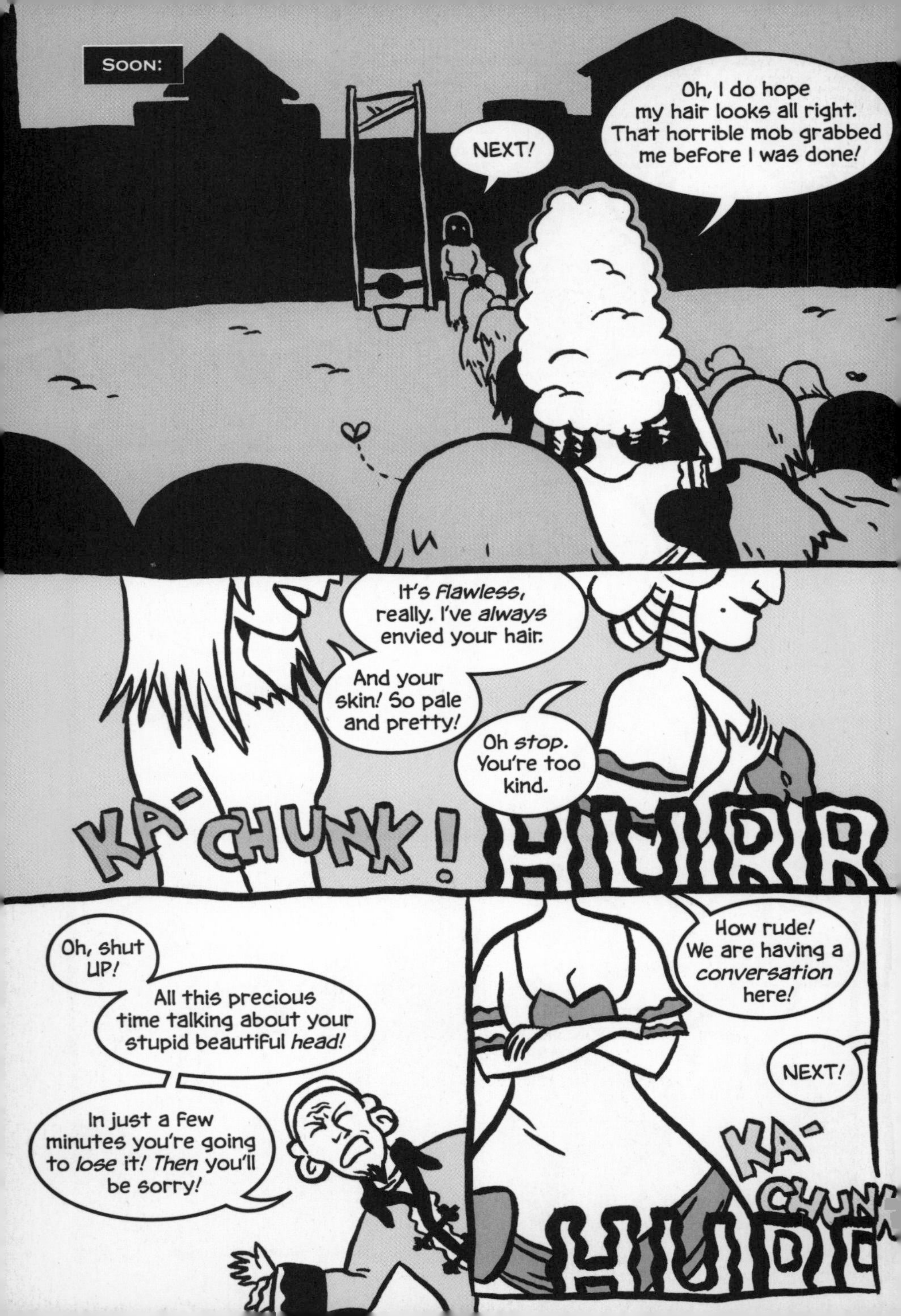
Soon:
NEXT!
Oh, I do hope my hair looks all right. That horrible mob grabbed me before I was done!
It's *flawless*, really. I've *always* envied your hair.
And your skin! So pale and pretty!
Oh *stop*. You're too kind.
KA-CHUNK!
HUURR
Oh, shut UP!
All this precious time talking about your stupid beautiful *head*!
In just a few minutes you're going to *lose* it! *Then* you'll be sorry!
How rude! We are having a *conversation* here!
NEXT!
KA-CHUNK

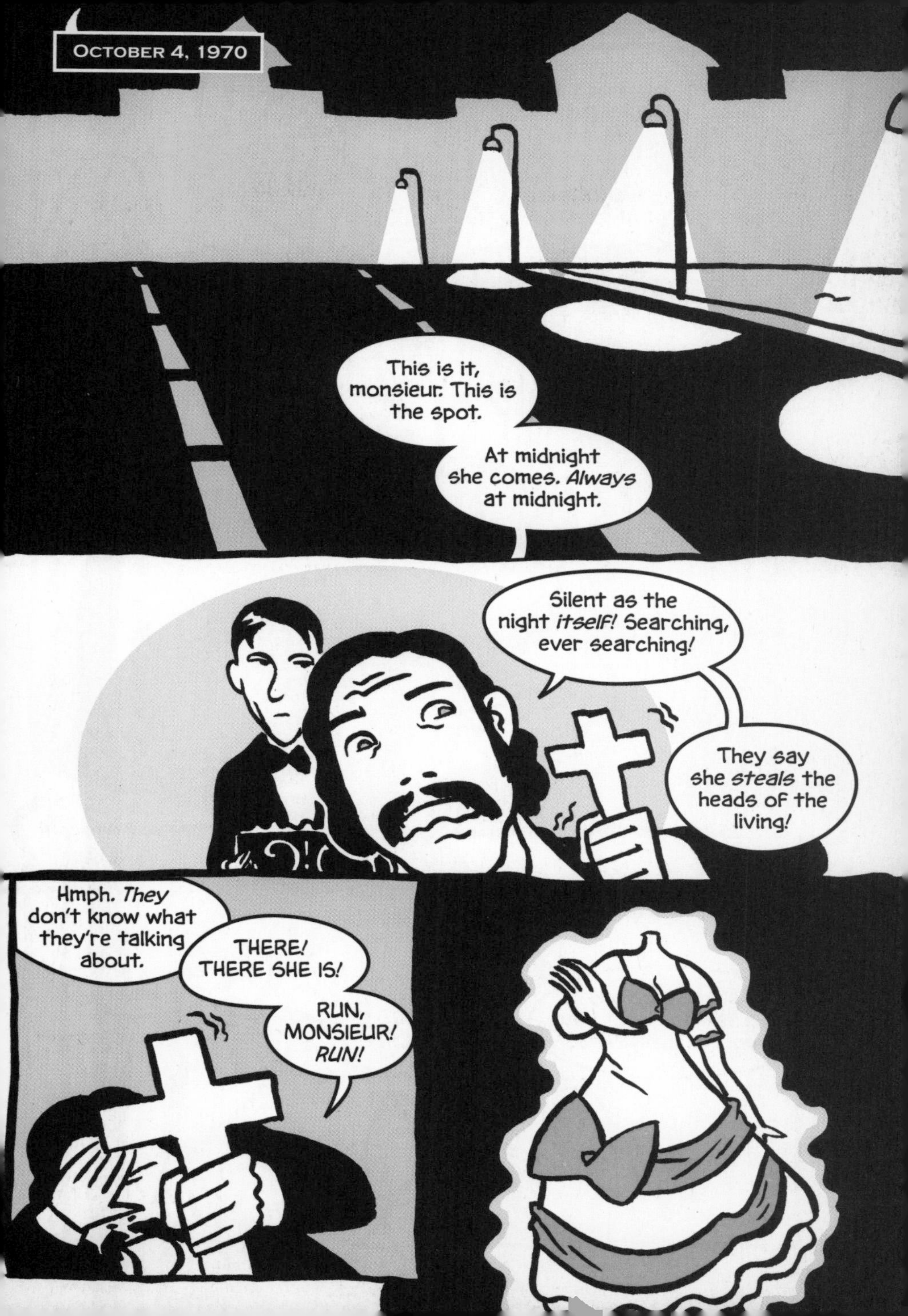
October 4, 1970
This is it, monsieur. This is the spot.
At midnight she comes. *Always* at midnight.
Silent as the night *itself!* Searching, ever searching!
They say she *steals* the heads of the living!
Hmph. *They* don't know what they're talking about.
THERE! THERE SHE IS!
RUN, MONSIEUR! *RUN!*

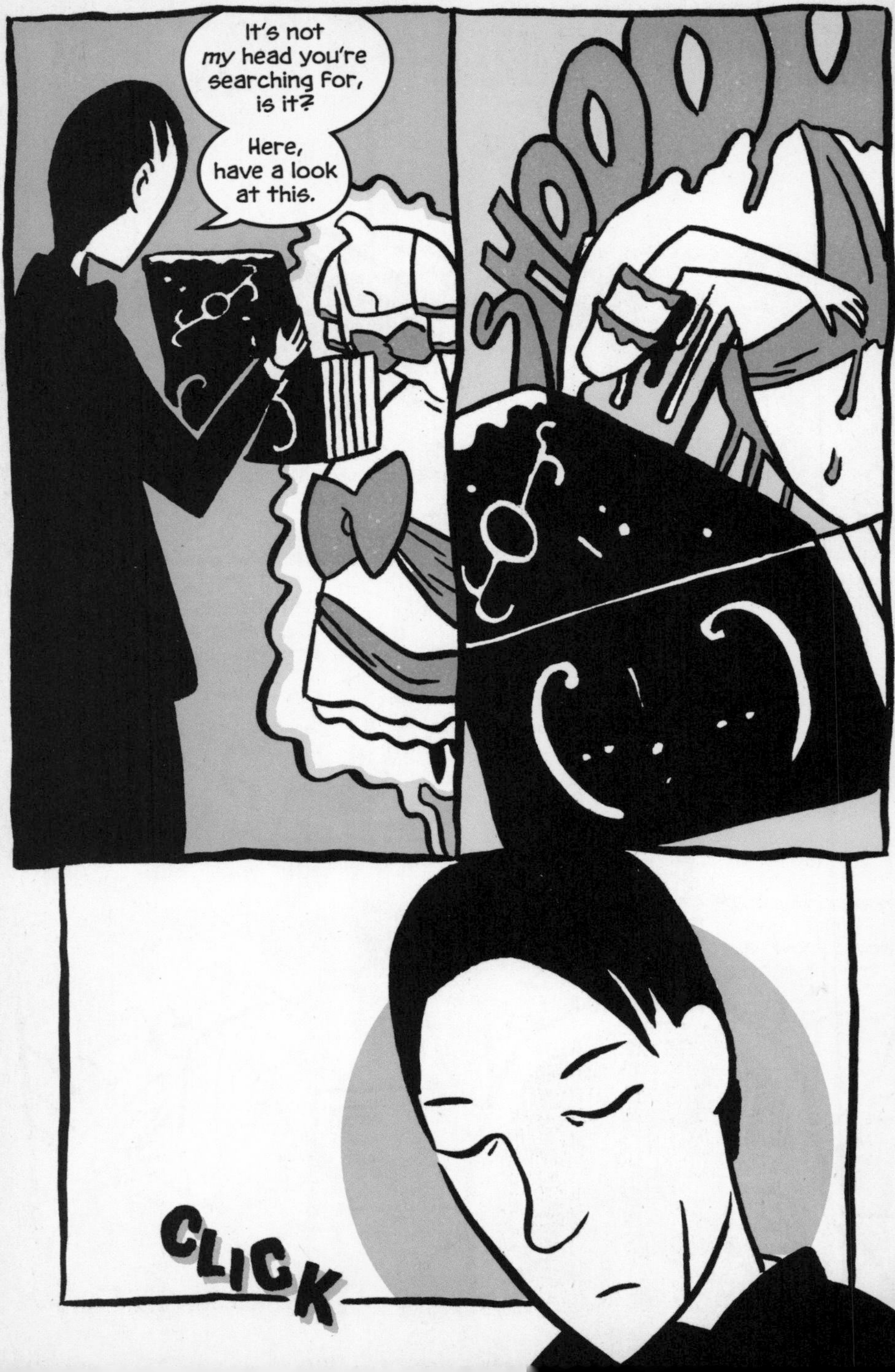
It's not *my* head you're searching for, is it?
Here, have a look at this.
SHOOOOO
CLICK

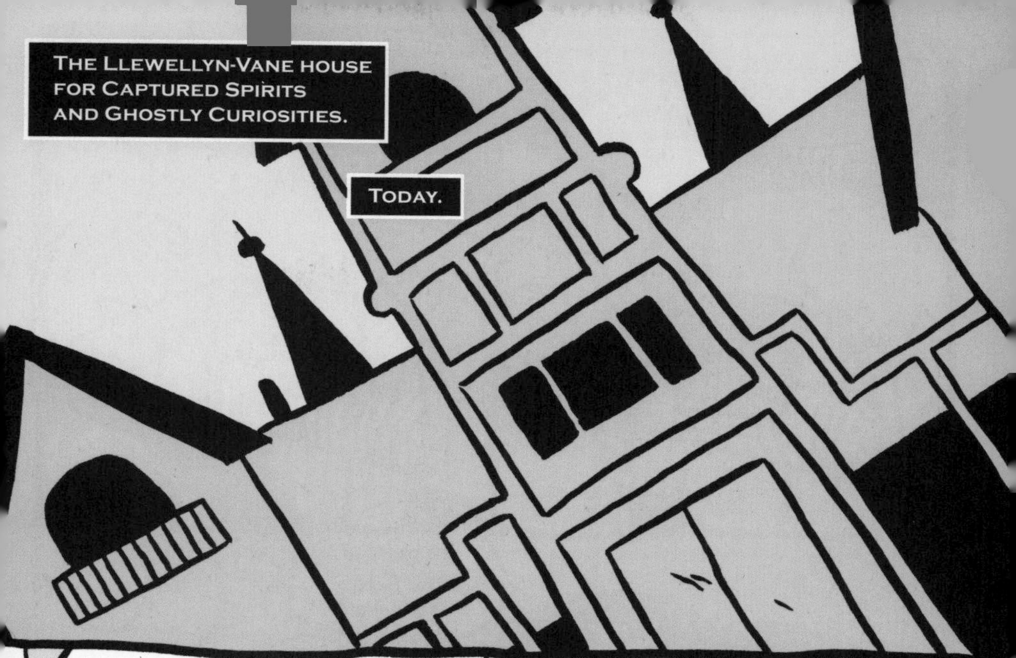
THE LLEWELLYN-VANE HOUSE FOR CAPTURED SPIRITS AND GHOSTLY CURIOSITIES.
TODAY.

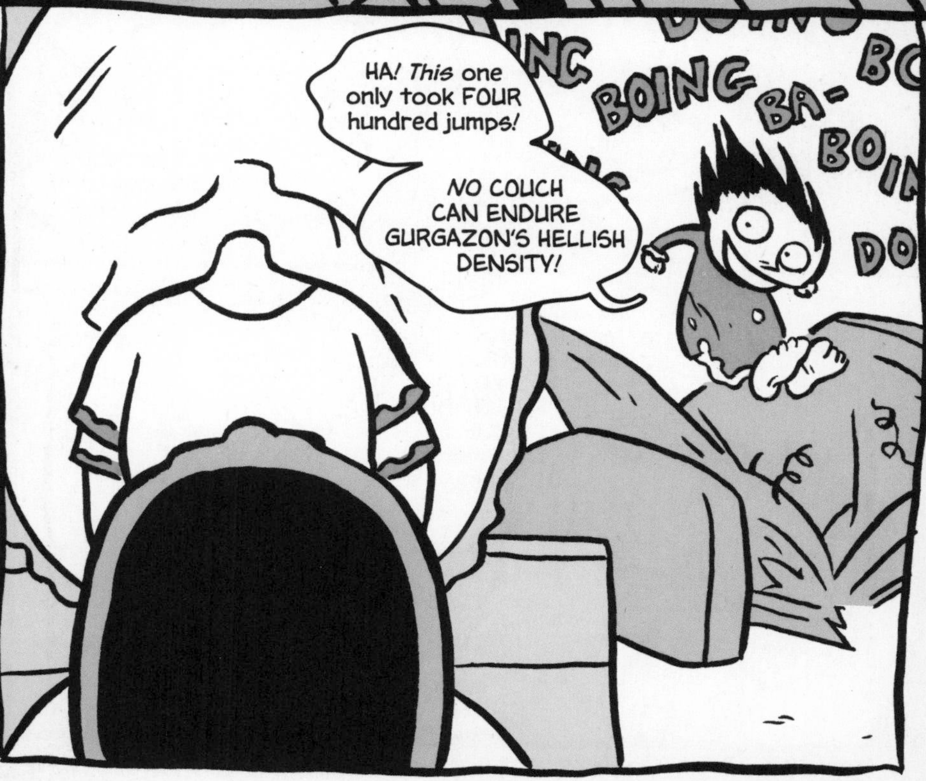
ING
BOING
BO
BA-
BOI
DO
HA! *This* one only took FOUR hundred jumps!
NO COUCH CAN ENDURE GURGAZON'S HELLISH DENSITY!

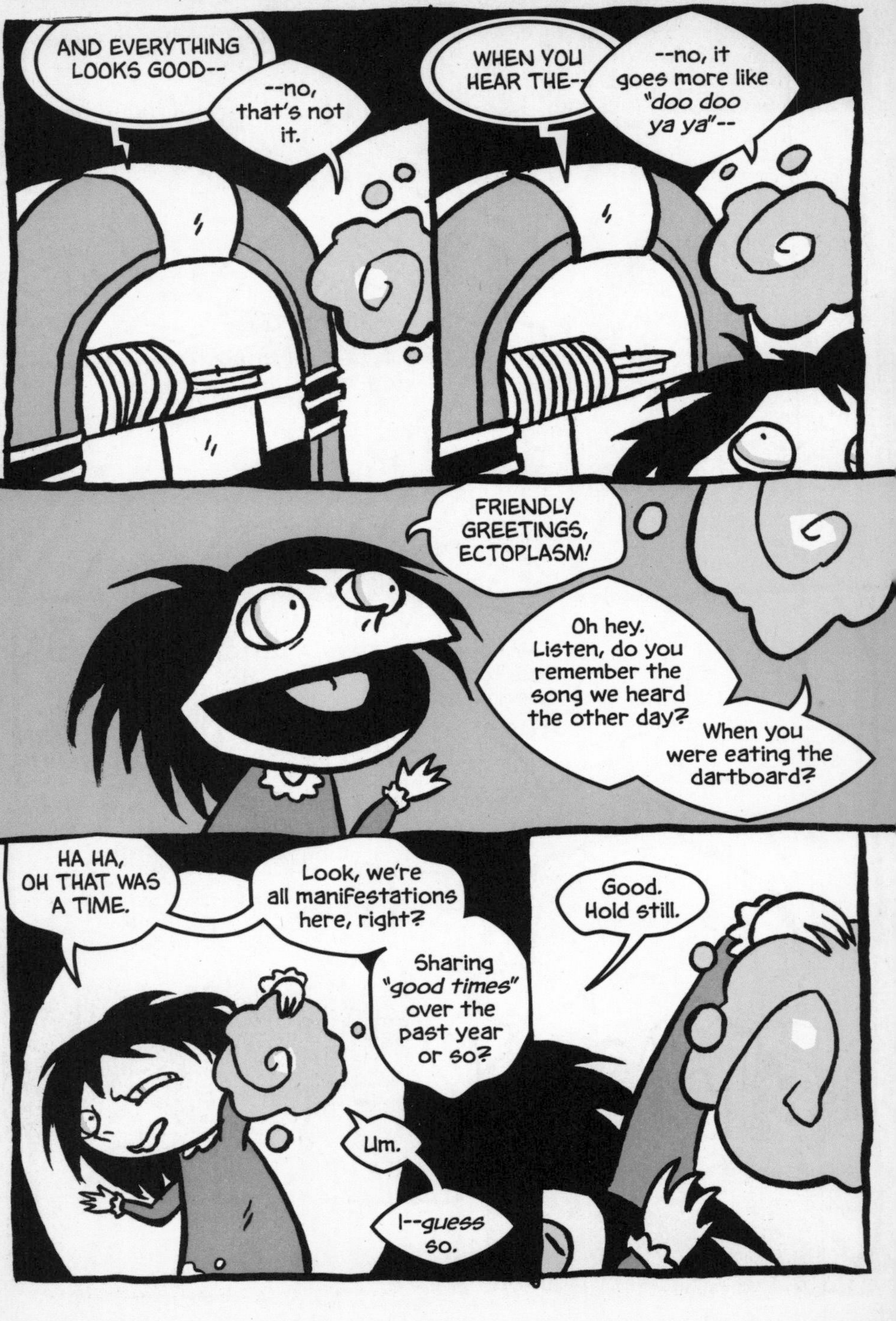
AND EVERYTHING LOOKS GOOD--
--no, that's not it.
WHEN YOU HEAR THE--
--no, it goes more like *"doo doo ya ya"*--
FRIENDLY GREETINGS, ECTOPLASM!
Oh hey. Listen, do you remember the song we heard the other day?
When you were eating the dartboard?
HA HA, OH THAT WAS A TIME.
Look, we're all manifestations here, right?
Sharing *"good times"* over the past year or so?
Um.
I--*guess* so.
Good. Hold still.

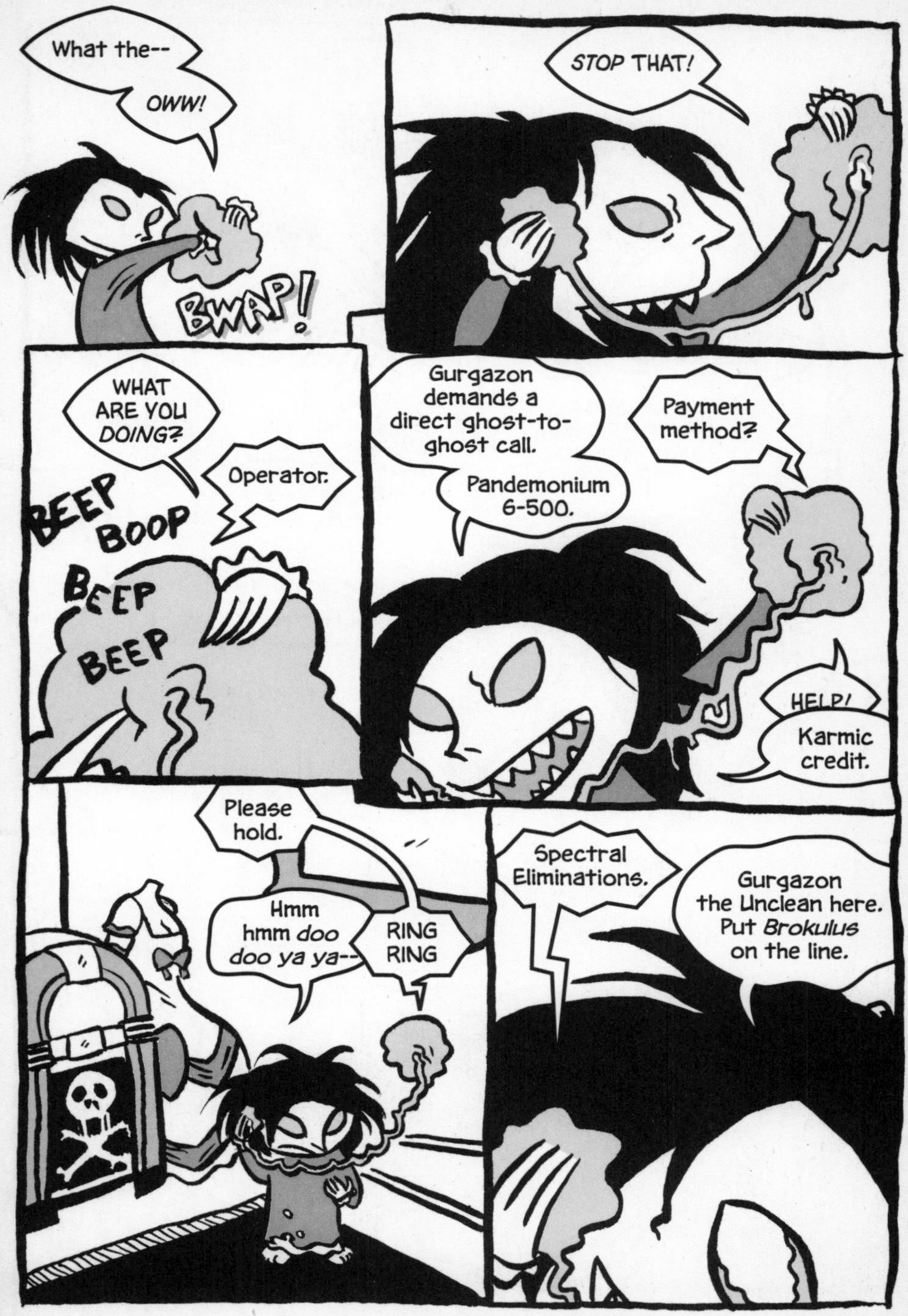
What the--
OWW!
BWAP!
STOP THAT!
WHAT ARE YOU DOING?
BEEP BOOP
BEEP BEEP
Operator.
Gurgazon demands a direct ghost-to-ghost call.
Pandemonium 6-500.
Payment method?
HELP!
Karmic credit.
Please hold.
Hmm hmm doo doo ya ya--
RING RING
Spectral Eliminations.
Gurgazon the Unclean here. Put Brokulus on the line.

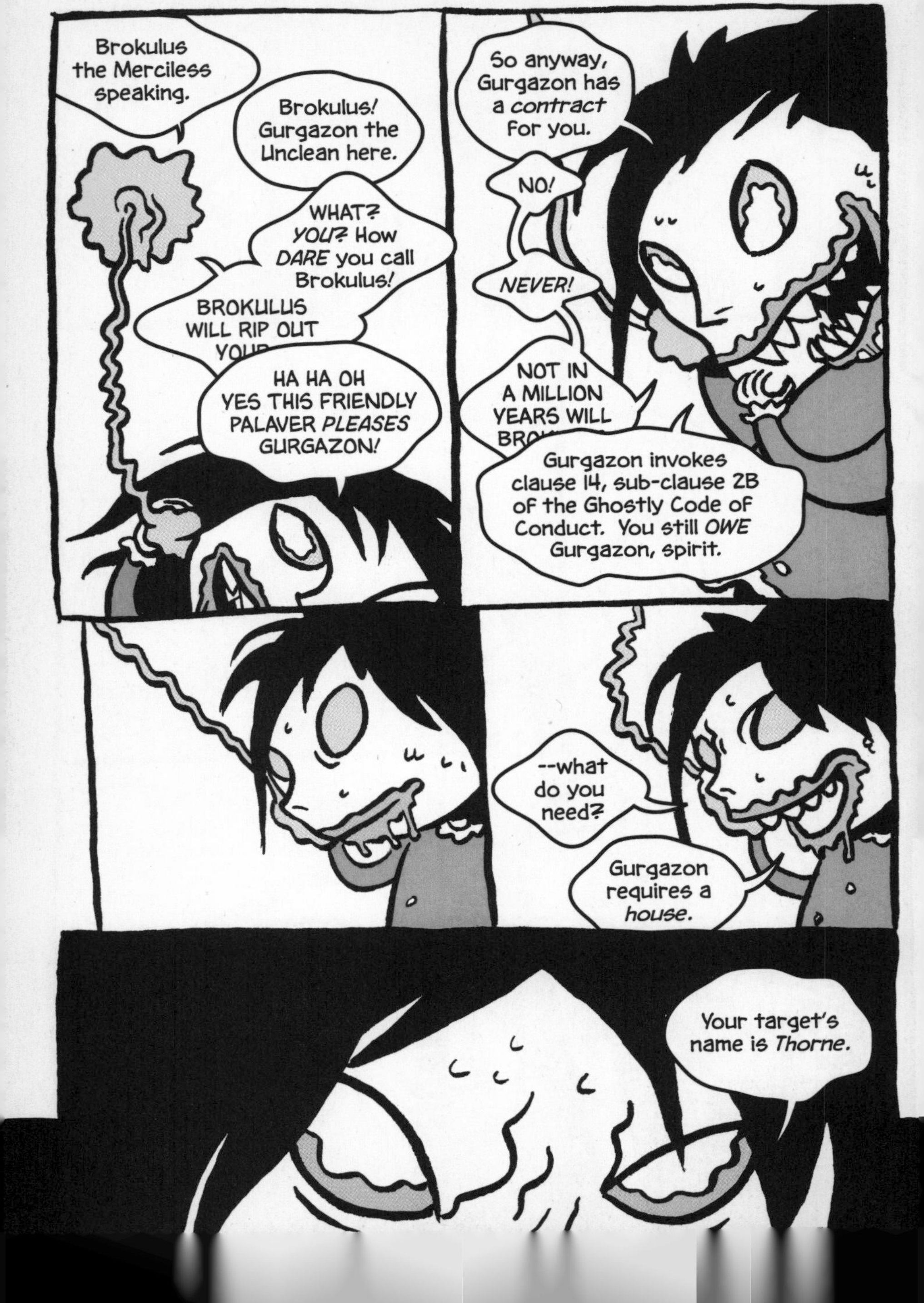
Brokulus the Merciless speaking.
Brokulus! Gurgazon the Unclean here.
WHAT? *YOU?* How *DARE* you call Brokulus!
BROKULUS WILL RIP OUT
HA HA OH YES THIS FRIENDLY PALAVER *PLEASES* GURGAZON!
So anyway, Gurgazon has a *contract* for you.
NO!
NEVER!
NOT IN A MILLION YEARS WILL
Gurgazon invokes clause 14, sub-clause 2B of the Ghostly Code of Conduct. You still *OWE* Gurgazon, spirit.
--what do you need?
Gurgazon requires a *house*.
Your target's name is *Thorne*.

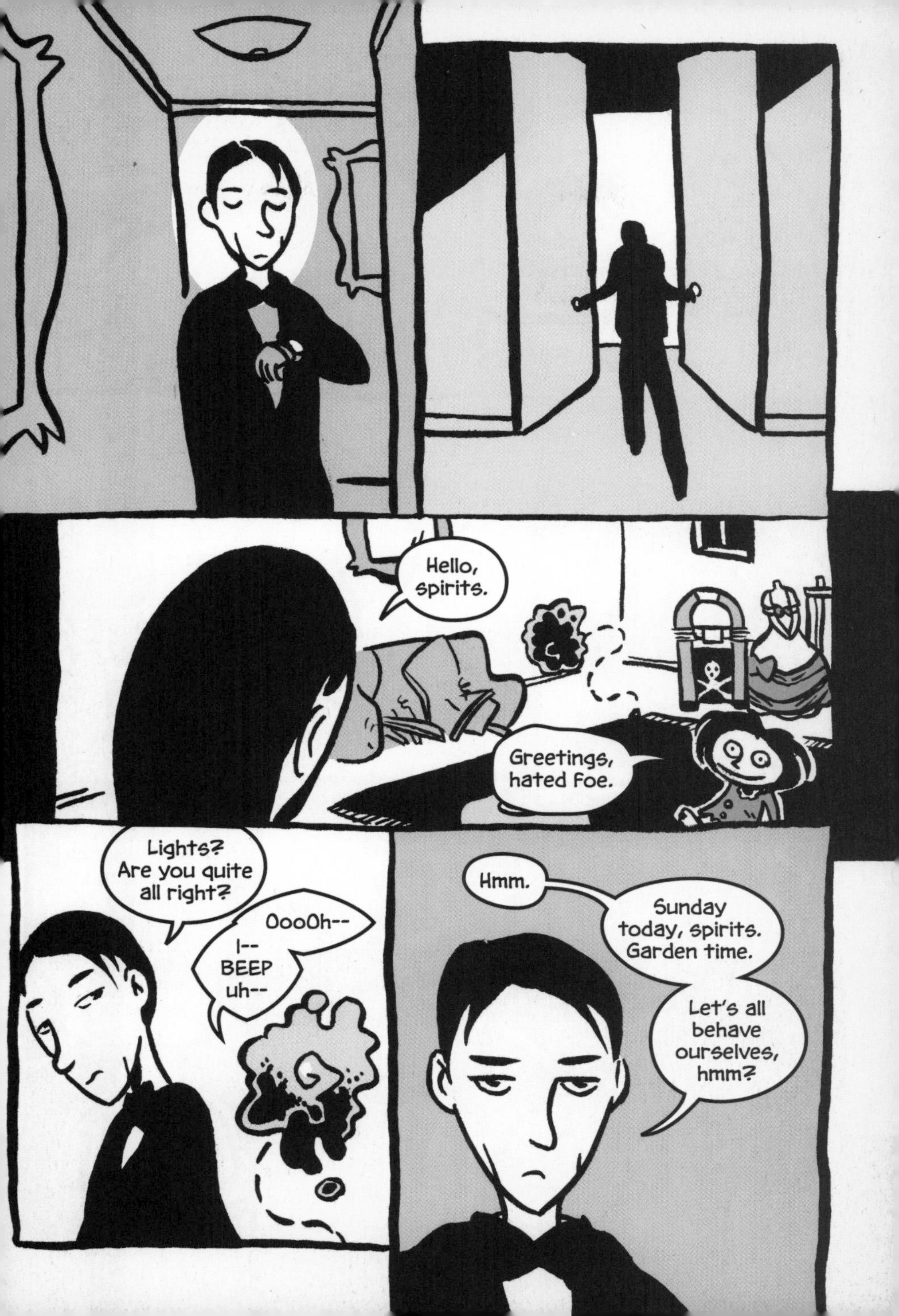
Hello, spirits.
Greetings, hated foe.
Lights? Are you quite all right?
OooOh--
I-- BEEP uh--
Hmm.
Sunday today, spirits. Garden time.
Let's all behave ourselves, hmm?

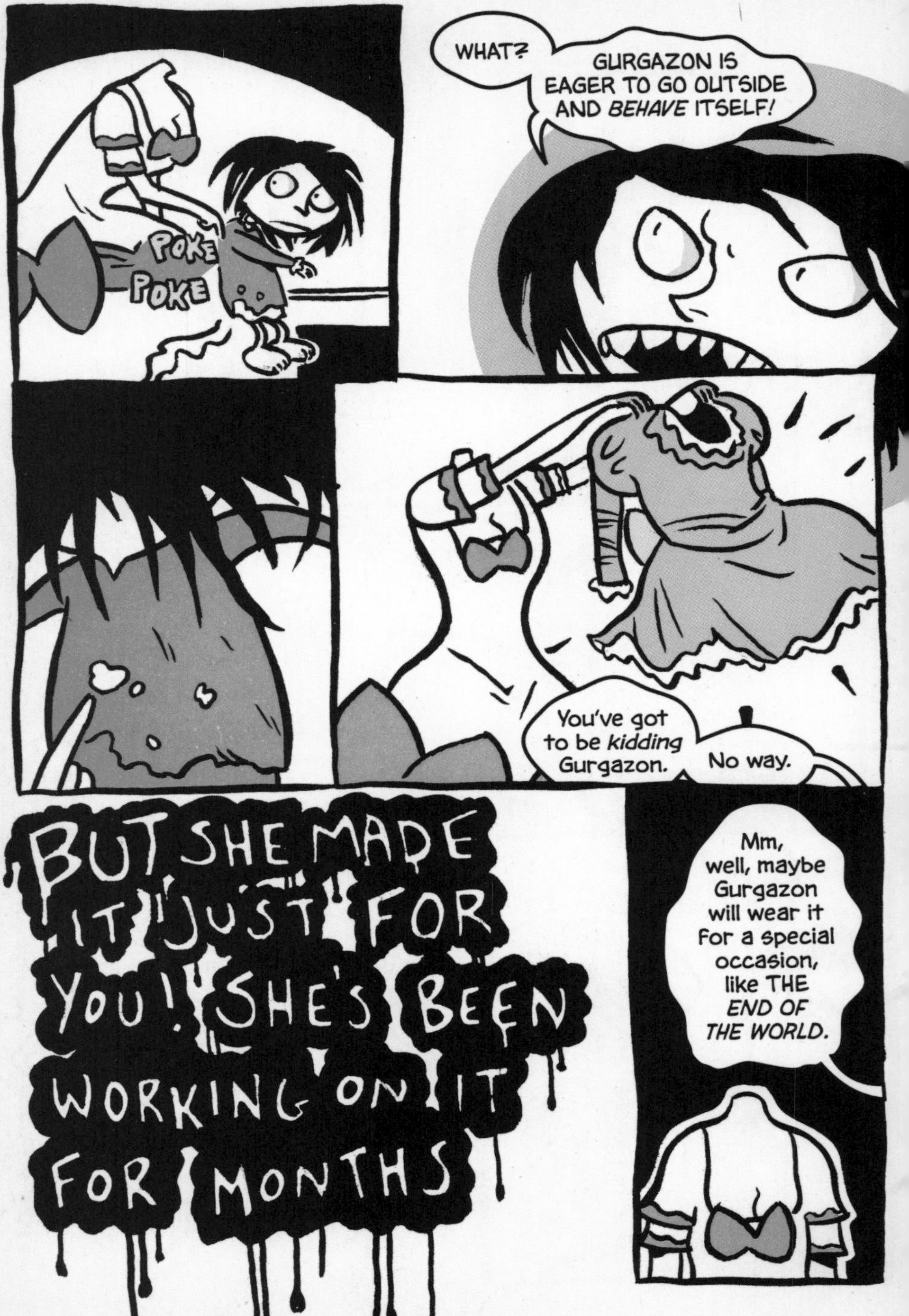
POKE
POKE
WHAT?
GURGAZON IS EAGER TO GO OUTSIDE AND *BEHAVE* ITSELF!
You've got to be *kidding* Gurgazon.
No way.
BUT SHE MADE IT JUST FOR YOU! SHE'S BEEN WORKING ON IT FOR MONTHS
Mm, well, maybe Gurgazon will wear it for a special occasion, like THE *END OF THE WORLD*.

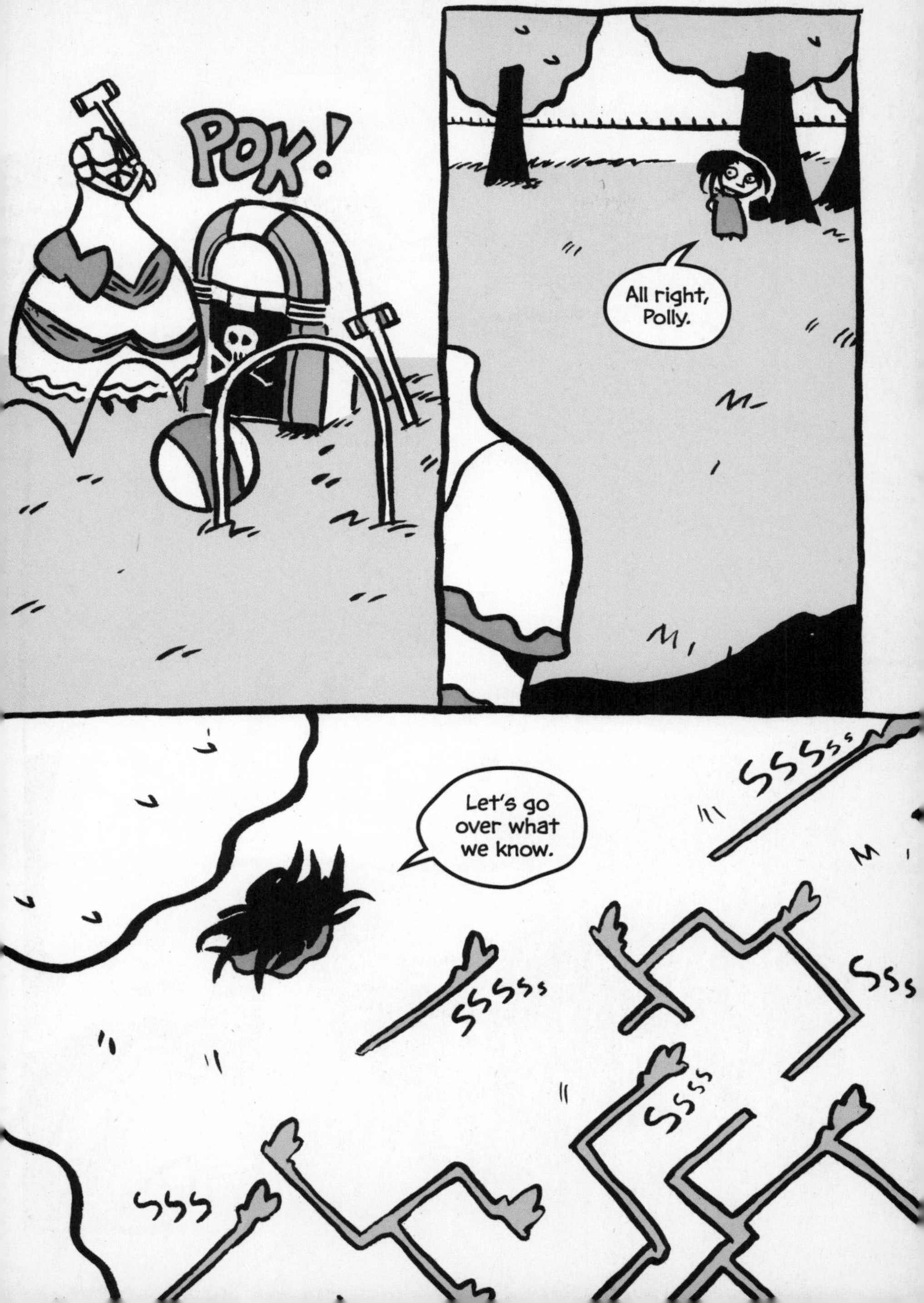
POK!
All right, Polly.
Let's go over what we know.
SSSss
SSSSs
SSs
SSSS
SSS

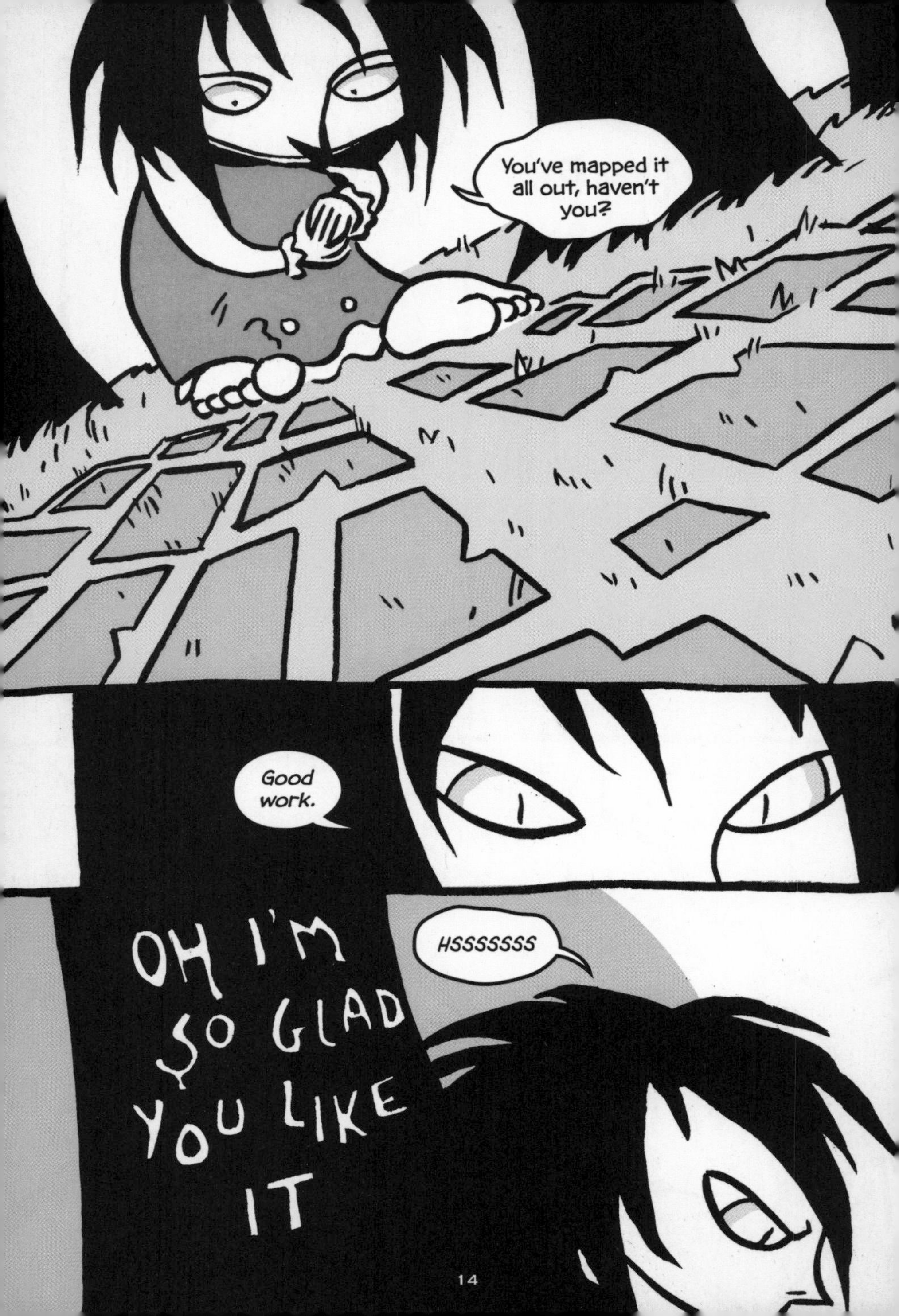

You've mapped it all out, haven't you?
Good work.
OH I'M SO GLAD YOU LIKE IT
HSSSSSSS

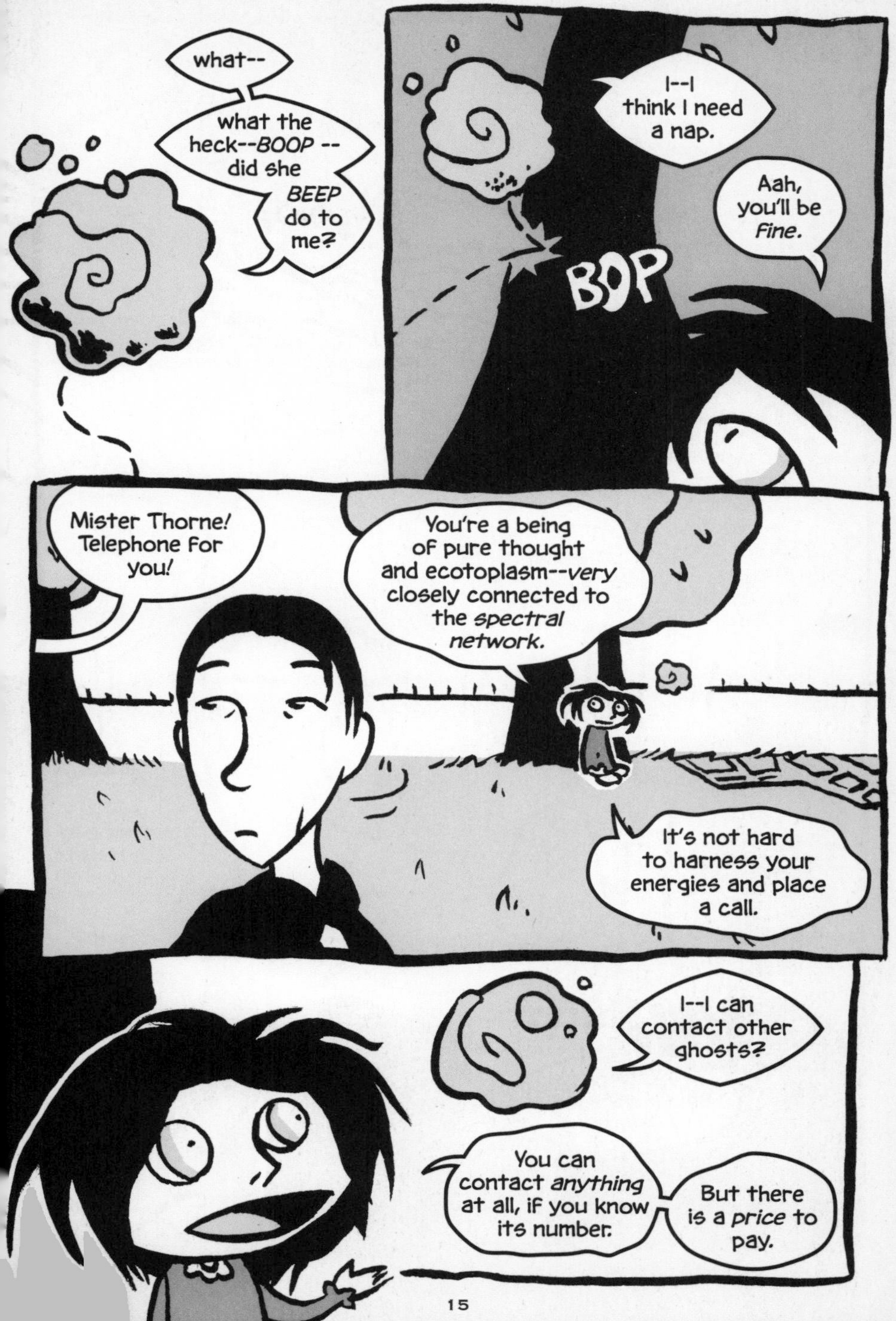
what--
what the heck--*BOOP* --did she *BEEP* do to me?
I--I think I need a nap.
BOP
Aah, you'll be *fine*.
Mister Thorne! Telephone for you!
You're a being of pure thought and ecotoplasm--*very* closely connected to the *spectral* network.
It's not hard to harness your energies and place a call.
I--I can contact other ghosts?
You can contact *anything* at all, if you know its number.
But there is a *price* to pay.

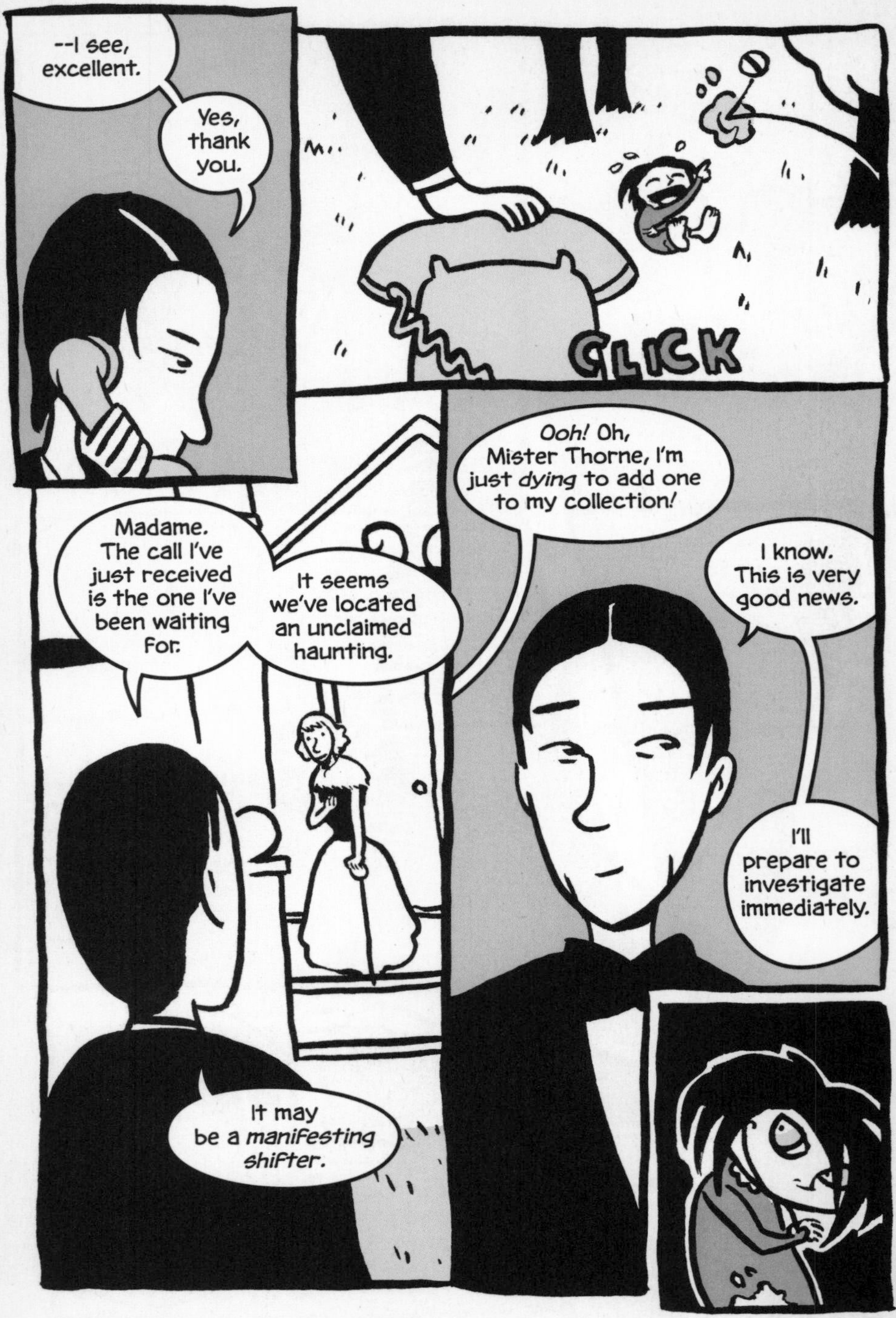
--I see, excellent.
Yes, thank you.
CLICK
Madame. The call I've just received is the one I've been waiting for.
It seems we've located an unclaimed haunting.
Ooh! Oh, Mister Thorne, I'm just dying to add one to my collection!
I know. This is very good news.
I'll prepare to investigate immediately.
It may be a manifesting shifter.

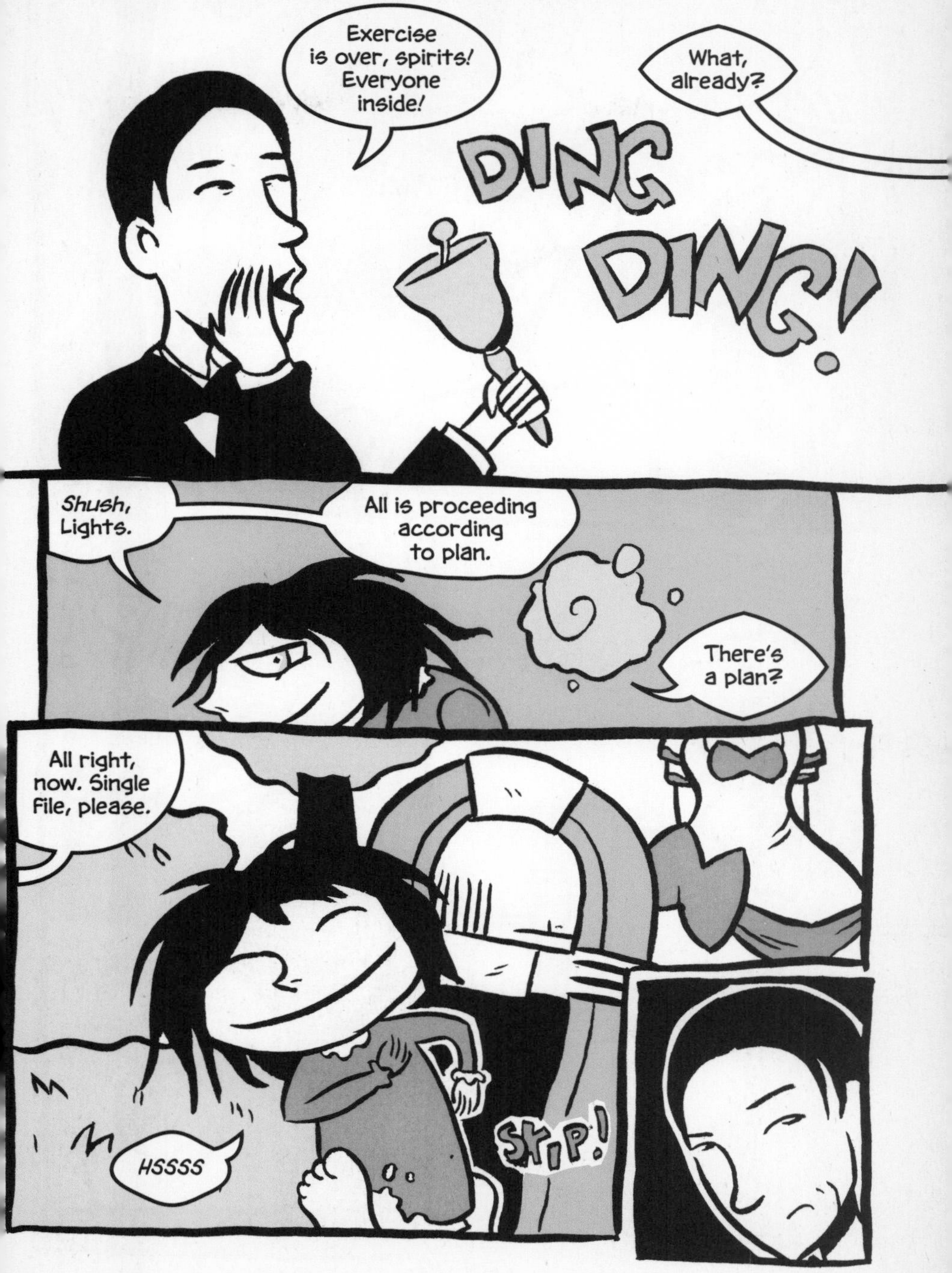
Exercise is over, spirits! Everyone inside!
What, already?
DING DING!
Shush, Lights.
All is proceeding according to plan.
There's a plan?
All right, now. Single file, please.
HSSSS
SKIP!

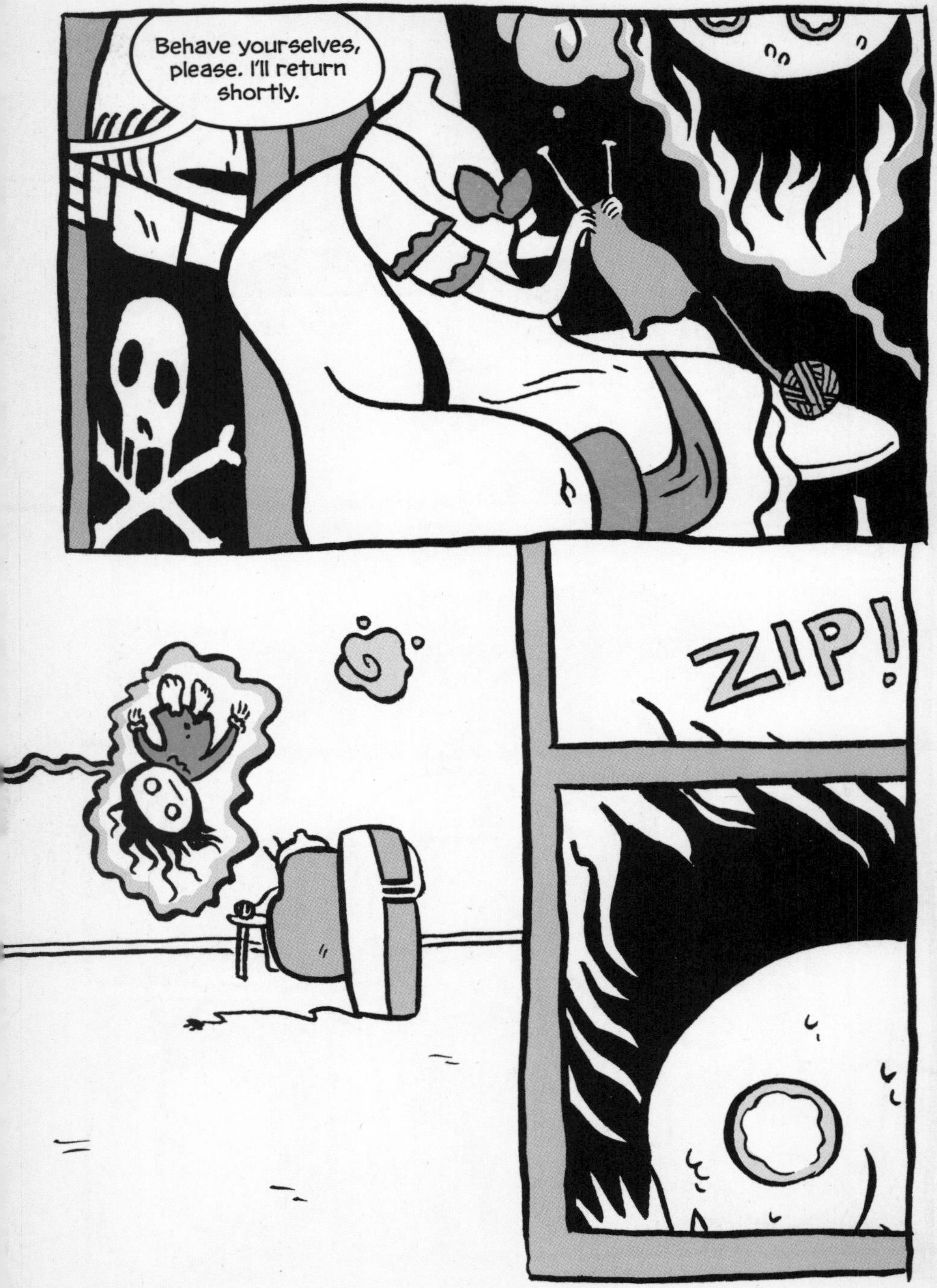
Behave yourselves, please. I'll return shortly.
ZIP!

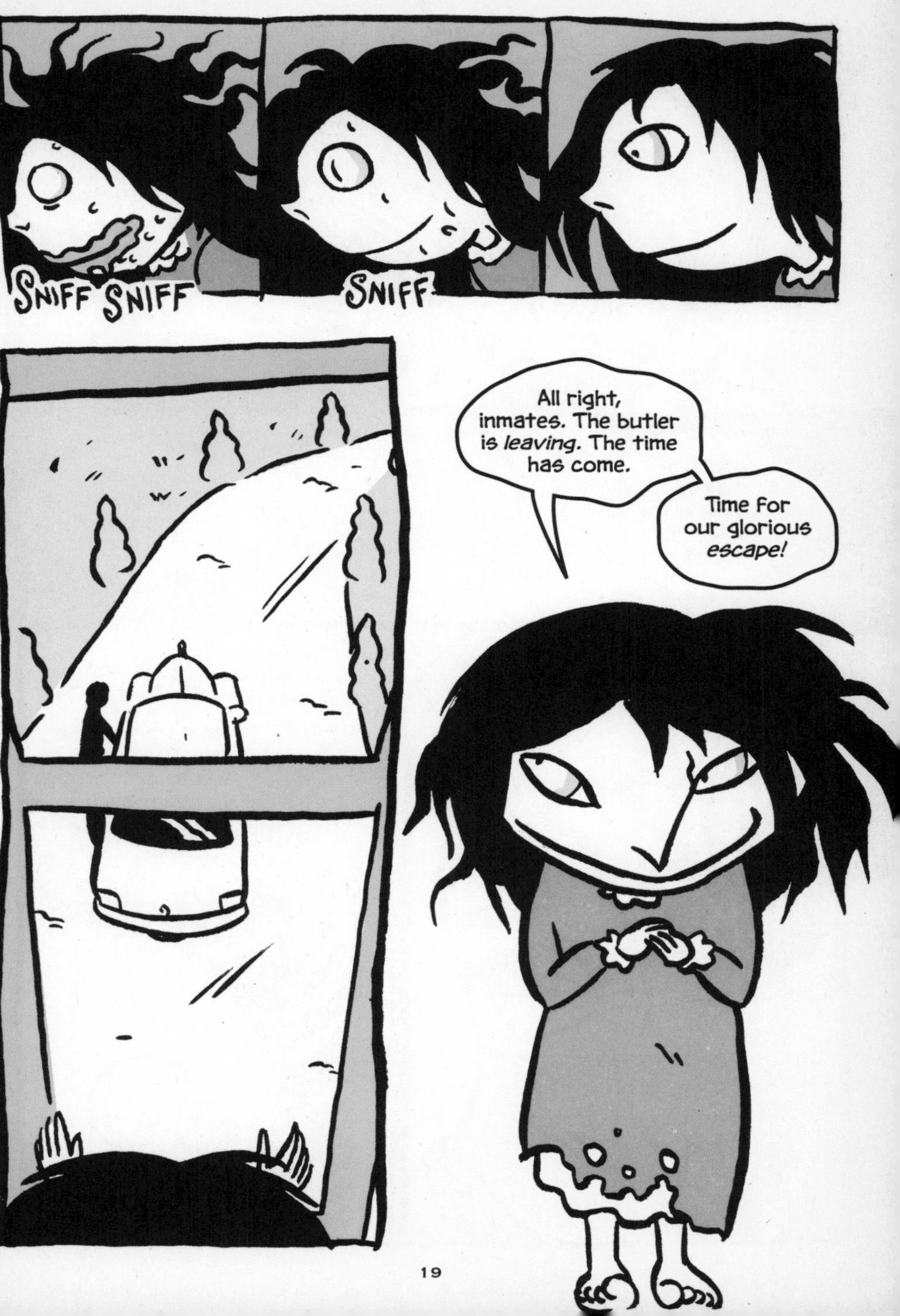
SNIFF SNIFF
SNIFF
All right, inmates. The butler is *leaving*. The time has come.
Time for our glorious *escape!*

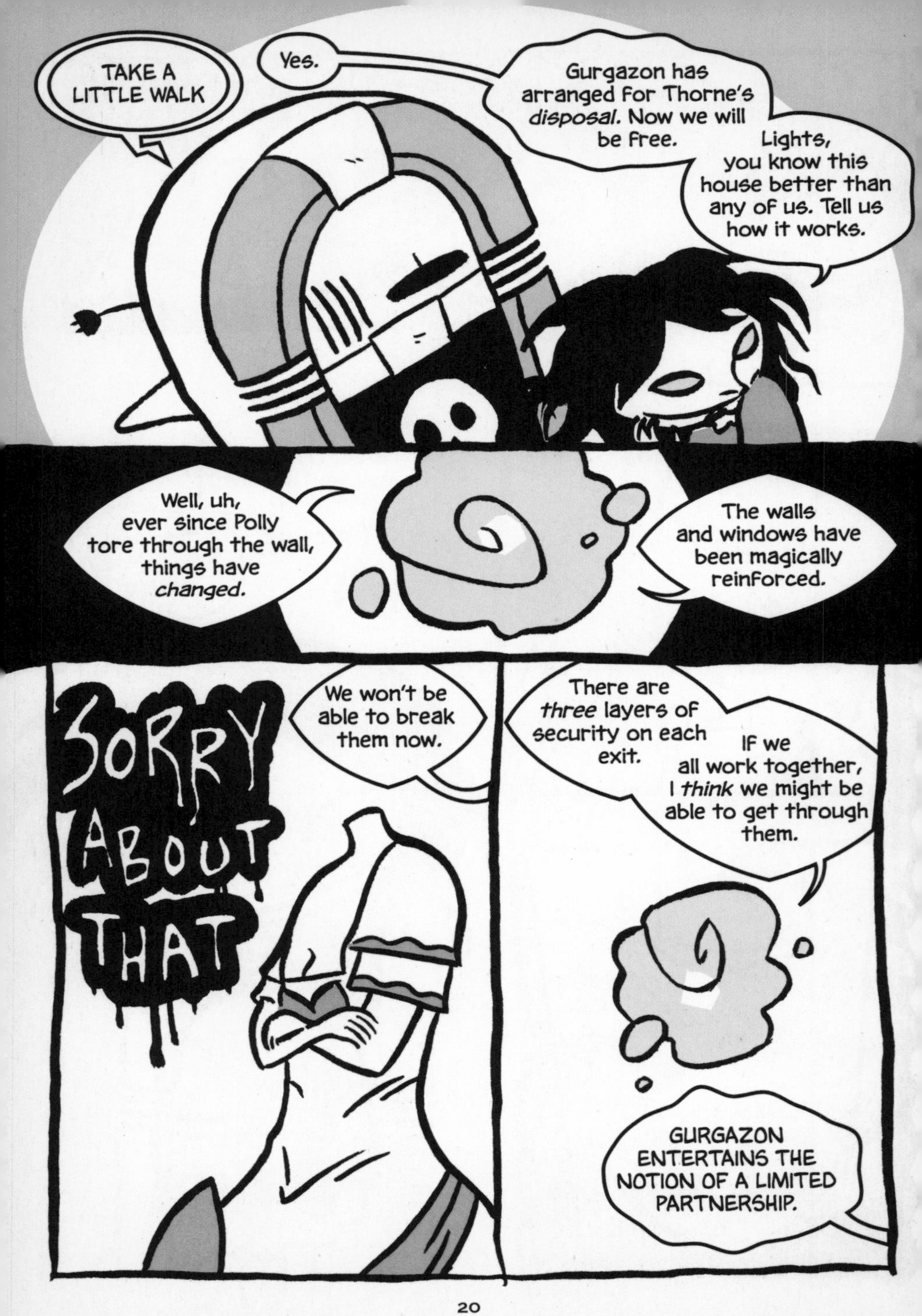
TAKE A LITTLE WALK
Yes.
Gurgazon has arranged for Thorne's *disposal*. Now we will be free.
Lights, you know this house better than any of us. Tell us how it works.
Well, uh, ever since Polly tore through the wall, things have *changed*.
The walls and windows have been magically reinforced.
SORRY ABOUT THAT
We won't be able to break them now.
There are *three* layers of security on each exit.
If we all work together, I *think* we might be able to get through them.
GURGAZON ENTERTAINS THE NOTION OF A LIMITED PARTNERSHIP.

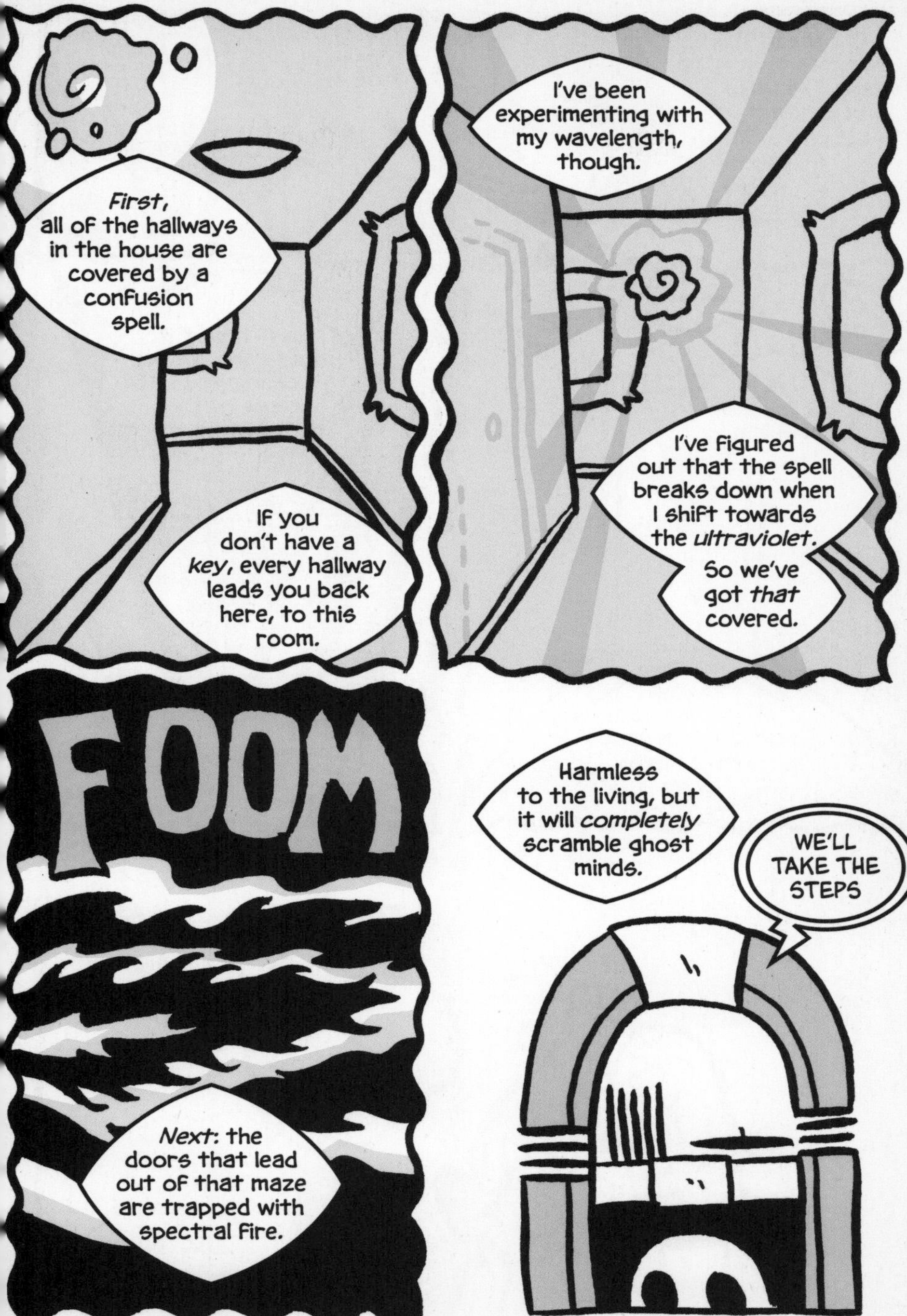
First, all of the hallways in the house are covered by a confusion spell.
If you don't have a *key*, every hallway leads you back here, to this room.
I've been experimenting with my wavelength, though.
I've figured out that the spell breaks down when I shift towards the *ultraviolet*.
So we've got *that* covered.
FOOM
Next: the doors that lead out of that maze are trapped with spectral fire.
Harmless to the living, but it will *completely* scramble ghost minds.
WE'LL TAKE THE STEPS

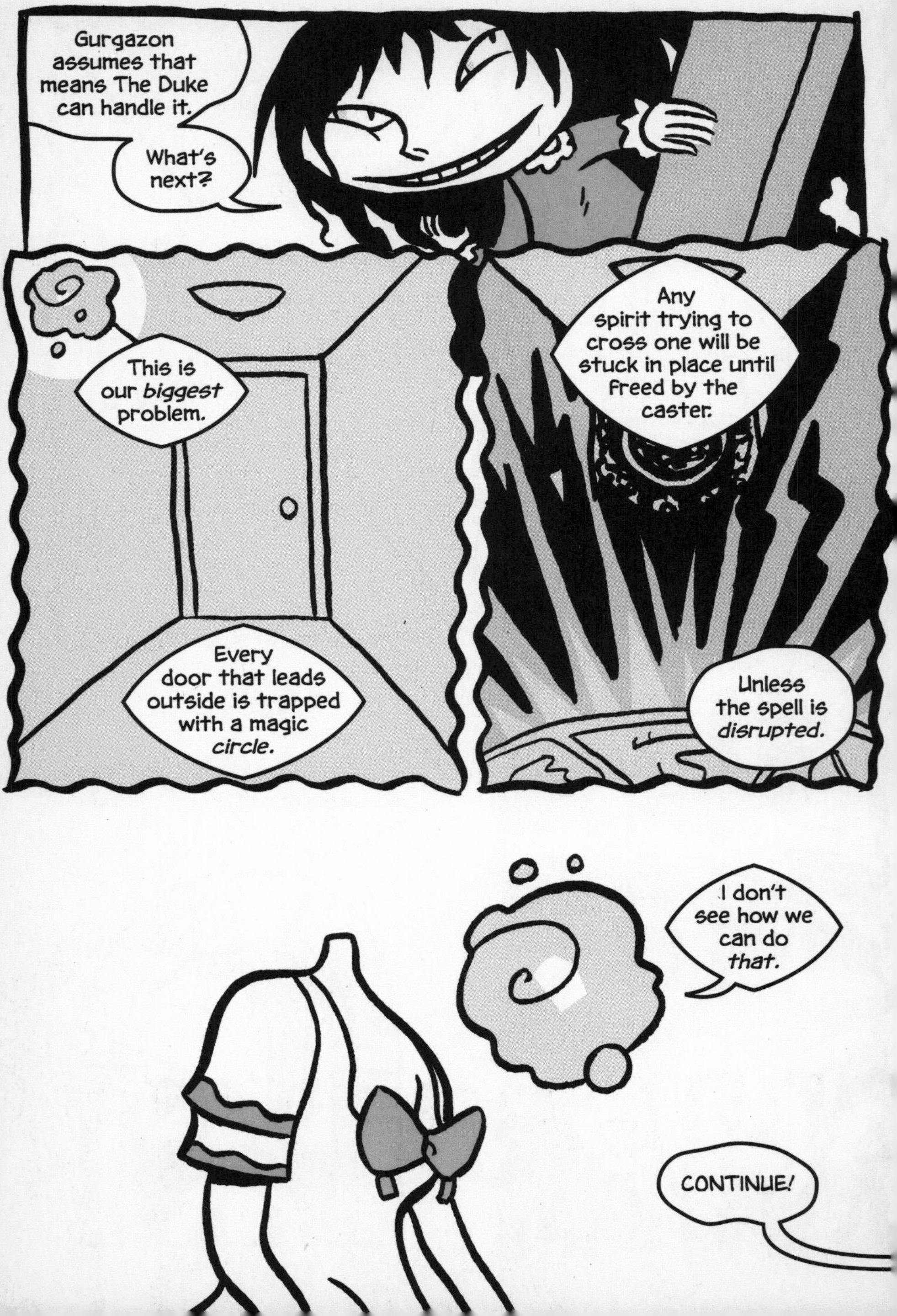

Gurgazon assumes that means The Duke can handle it.
What's next?
This is our *biggest* problem.
Every door that leads outside is trapped with a magic *circle*.
Any spirit trying to cross one will be stuck in place until freed by the caster.
Unless the spell is *disrupted*.
I don't see how we can do *that*.
CONTINUE!

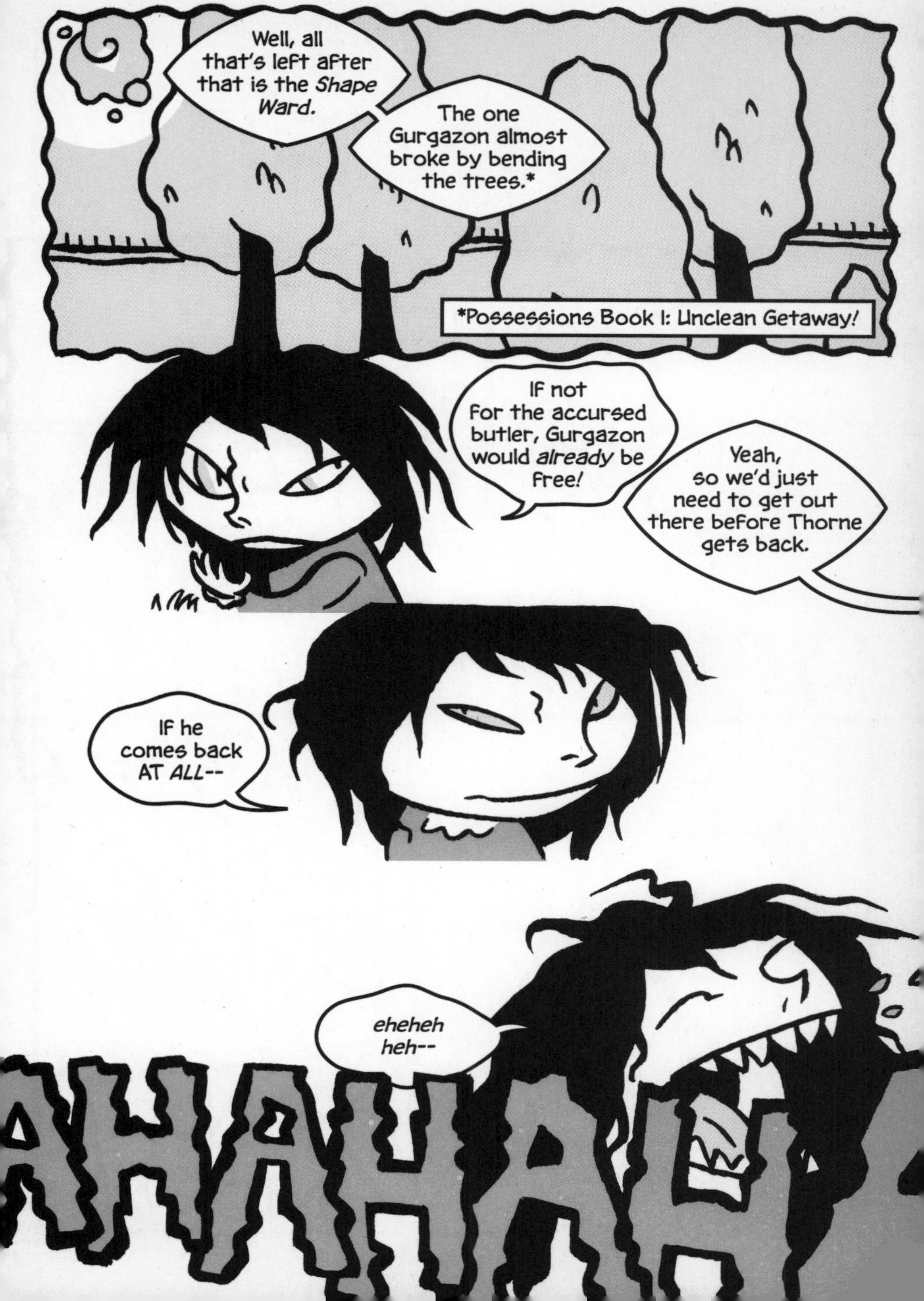
Well, all that's left after that is the *Shape Ward*.
The one Gurgazon almost broke by bending the trees.*
*Possessions Book 1: Unclean Getaway!
If not for the accursed butler, Gurgazon would *already* be free!
Yeah, so we'd just need to get out there before Thorne gets back.
If he comes back AT *ALL*--
eheheh heh--
AHAHAH

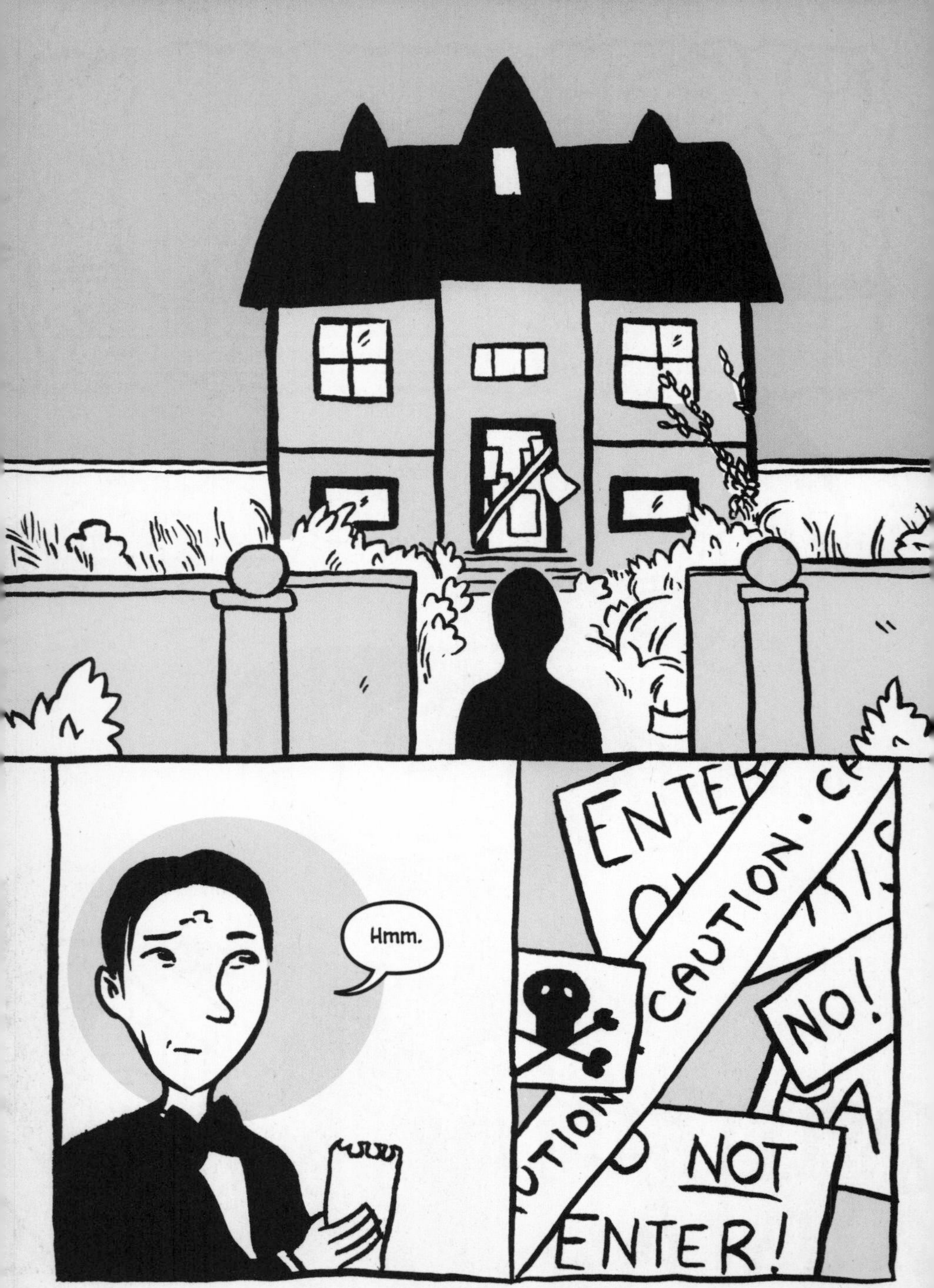
Hmm.
CAUTION.
NO!
NOT
ENTER!

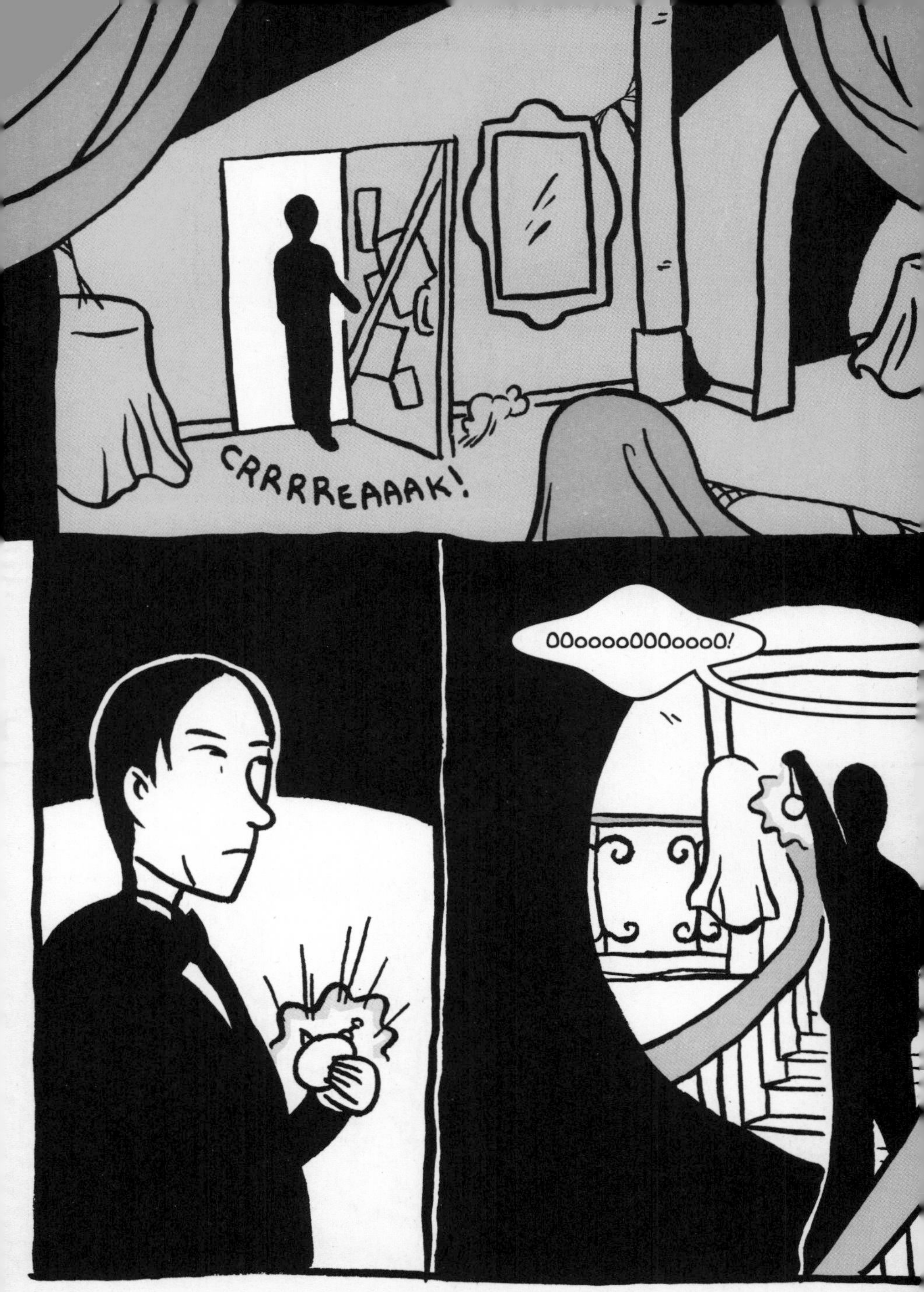
CRRRREAAAK!
OOoooooOOOooooO!

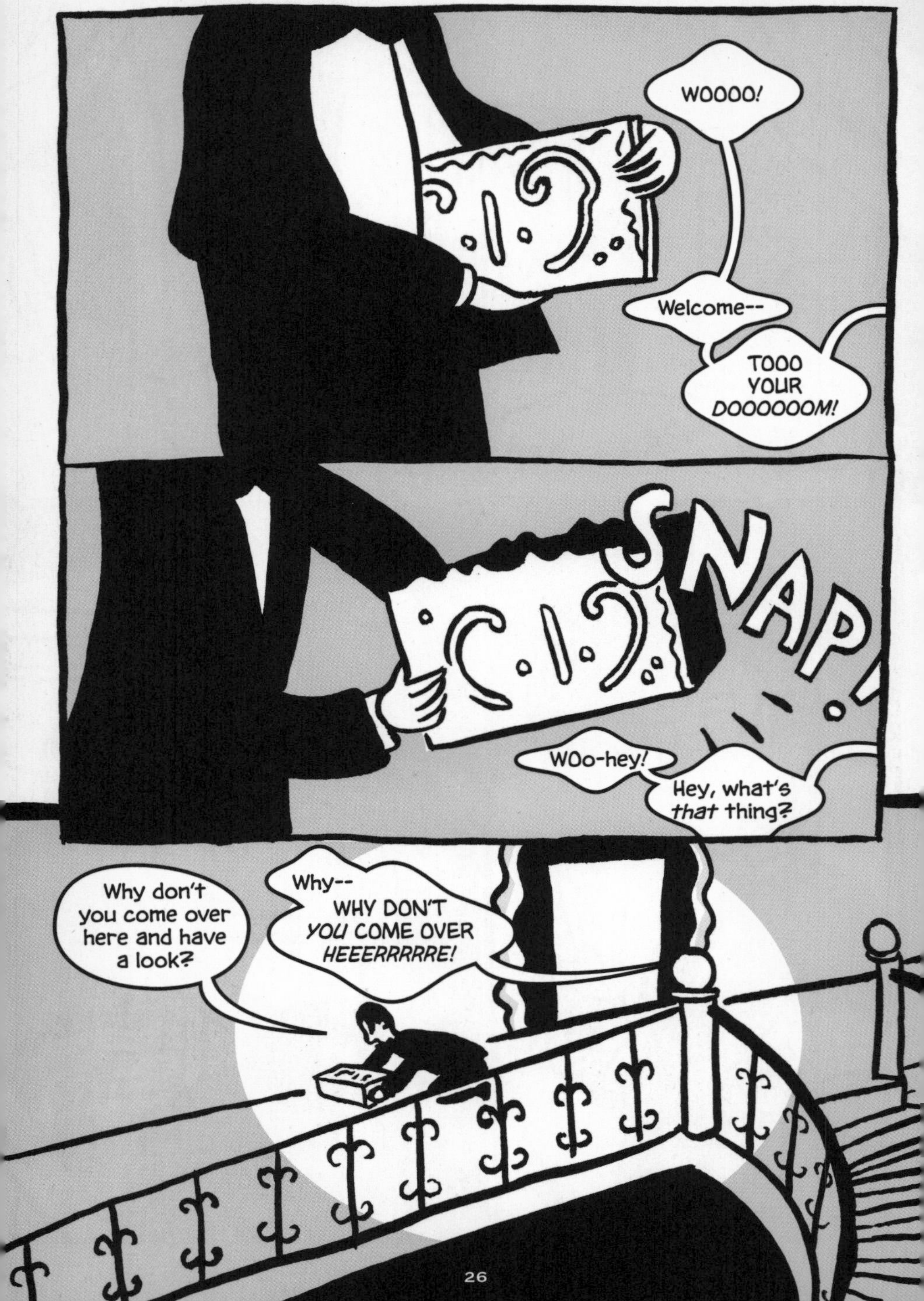
WOOOO!
Welcome--
TOOO YOUR DOOOOOOM!
SNAP!
WOo-hey!
Hey, what's that thing?
Why don't you come over here and have a look?
Why--
WHY DON'T YOU COME OVER HEEERRRRRE!

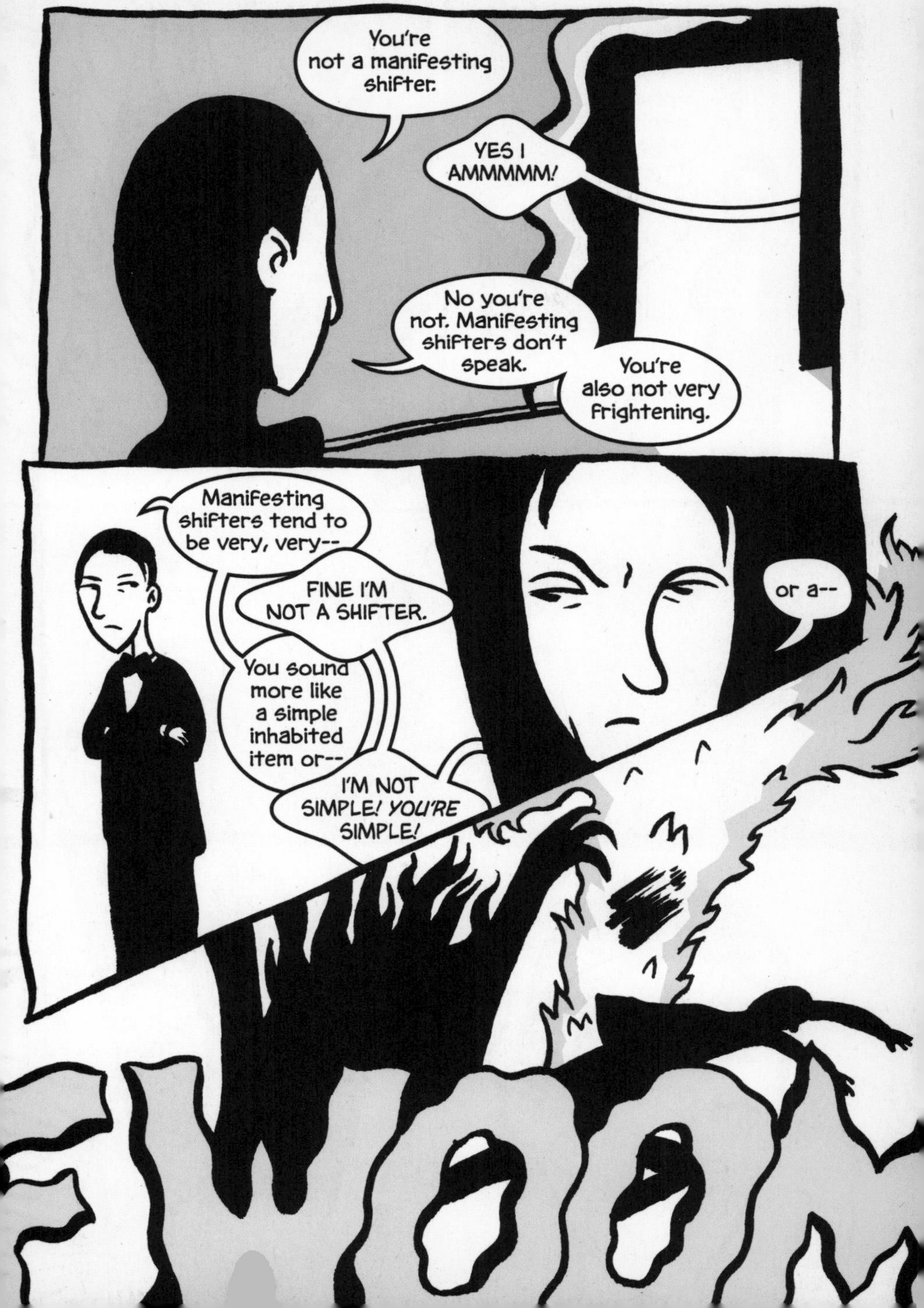

You're not a manifesting shifter.
YES I AMMMMM!
No you're not. Manifesting shifters don't speak.
You're also not very frightening.
Manifesting shifters tend to be very, very--
FINE I'M NOT A SHIFTER.
You sound more like a simple inhabited item or--
I'M NOT SIMPLE! *YOU'RE* SIMPLE!
or a--

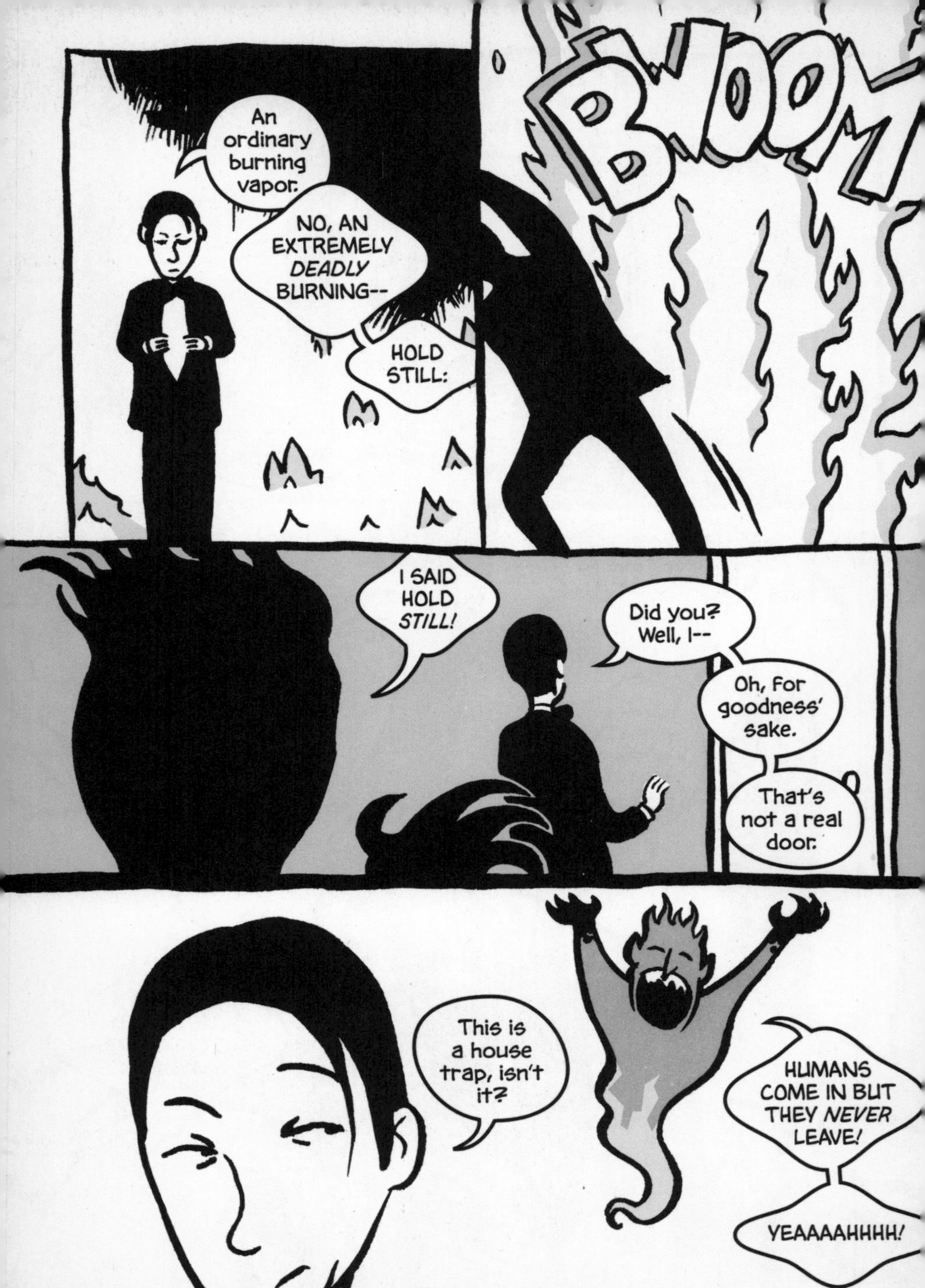
BWOOM
An ordinary burning vapor.
NO, AN EXTREMELY *DEADLY* BURNING--
HOLD STILL:
I SAID HOLD *STILL!*
Did you? Well, I--
Oh, for goodness' sake.
That's not a real door.
This is a house trap, isn't it?
HUMANS COME IN BUT THEY *NEVER* LEAVE!
YEAAAAHHHH!

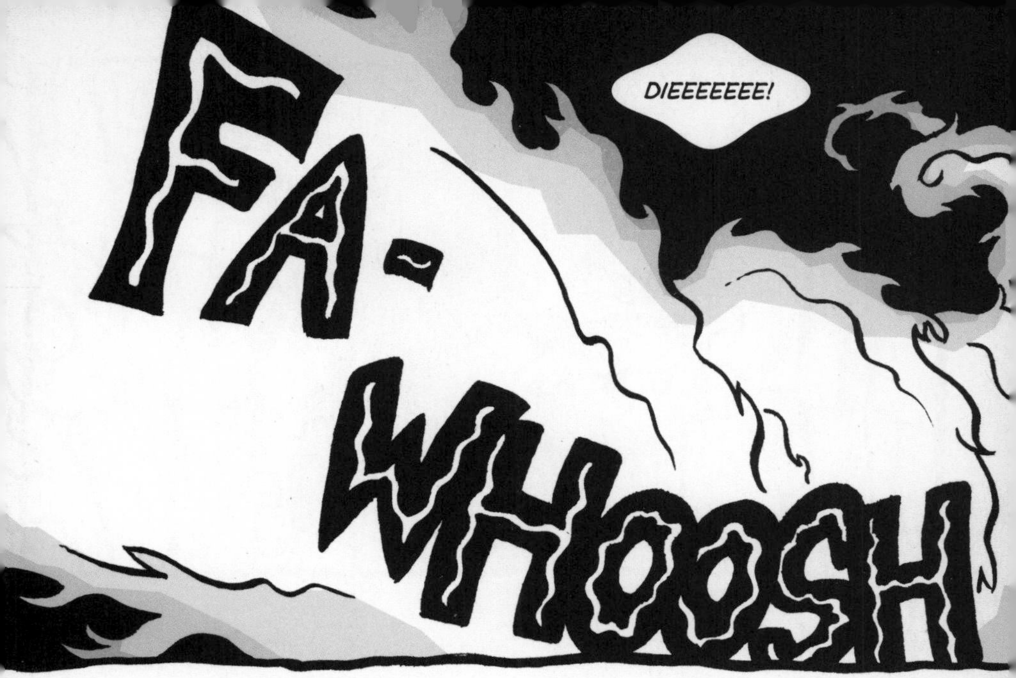
DIEEEEEEE!
FA-WHOOSH

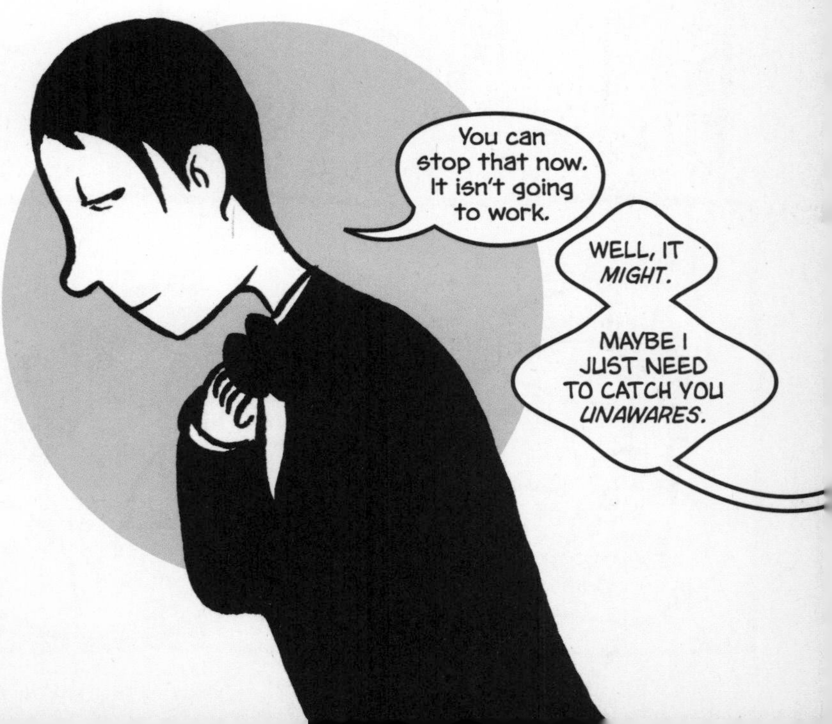
You can stop that now. It isn't going to work.
WELL, IT *MIGHT*.
MAYBE I JUST NEED TO CATCH YOU *UNAWARES*.

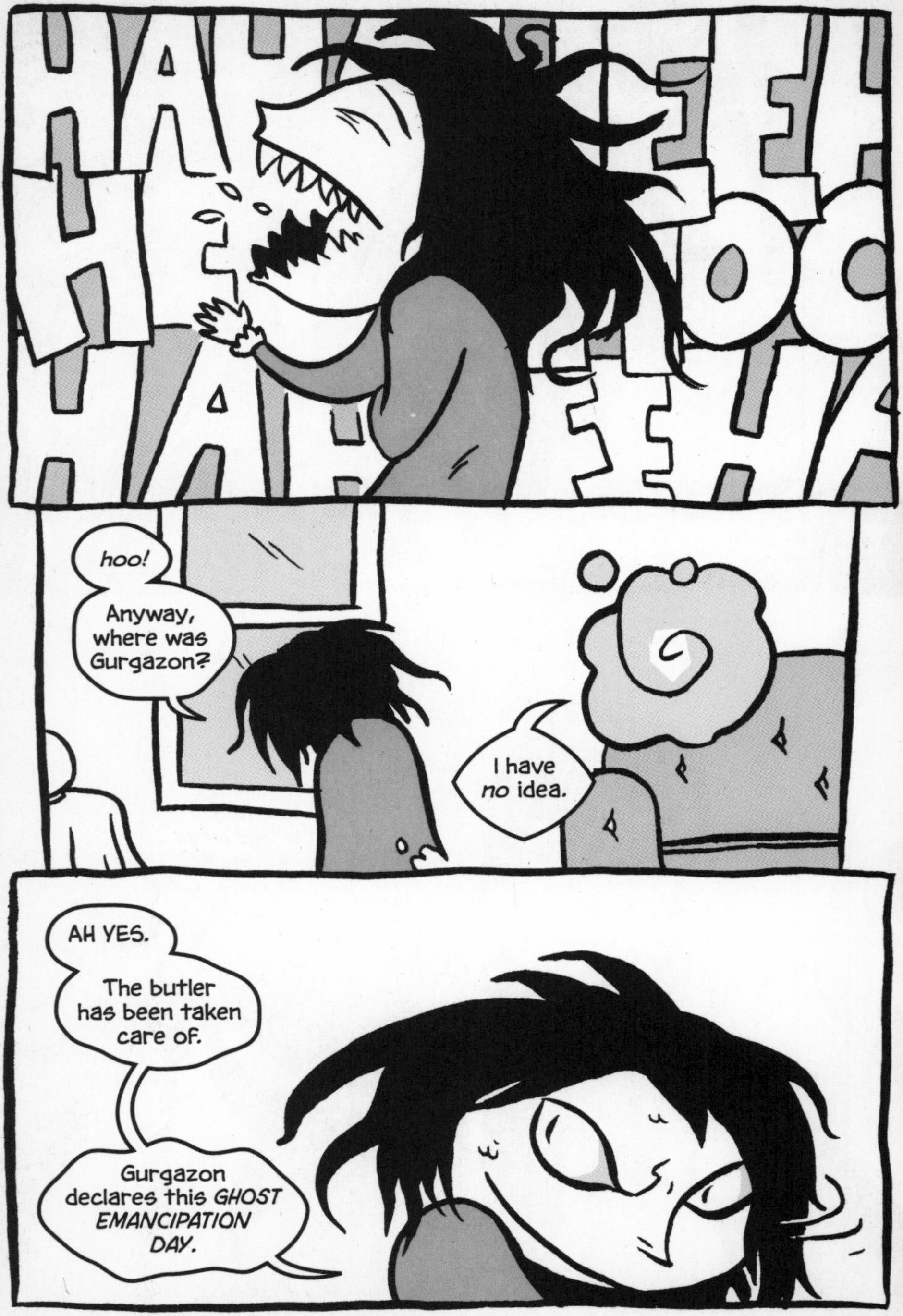
hoo!
Anyway, where was Gurgazon?
I have *no* idea.
AH YES.
The butler has been taken care of.
Gurgazon declares this *GHOST EMANCIPATION DAY*.

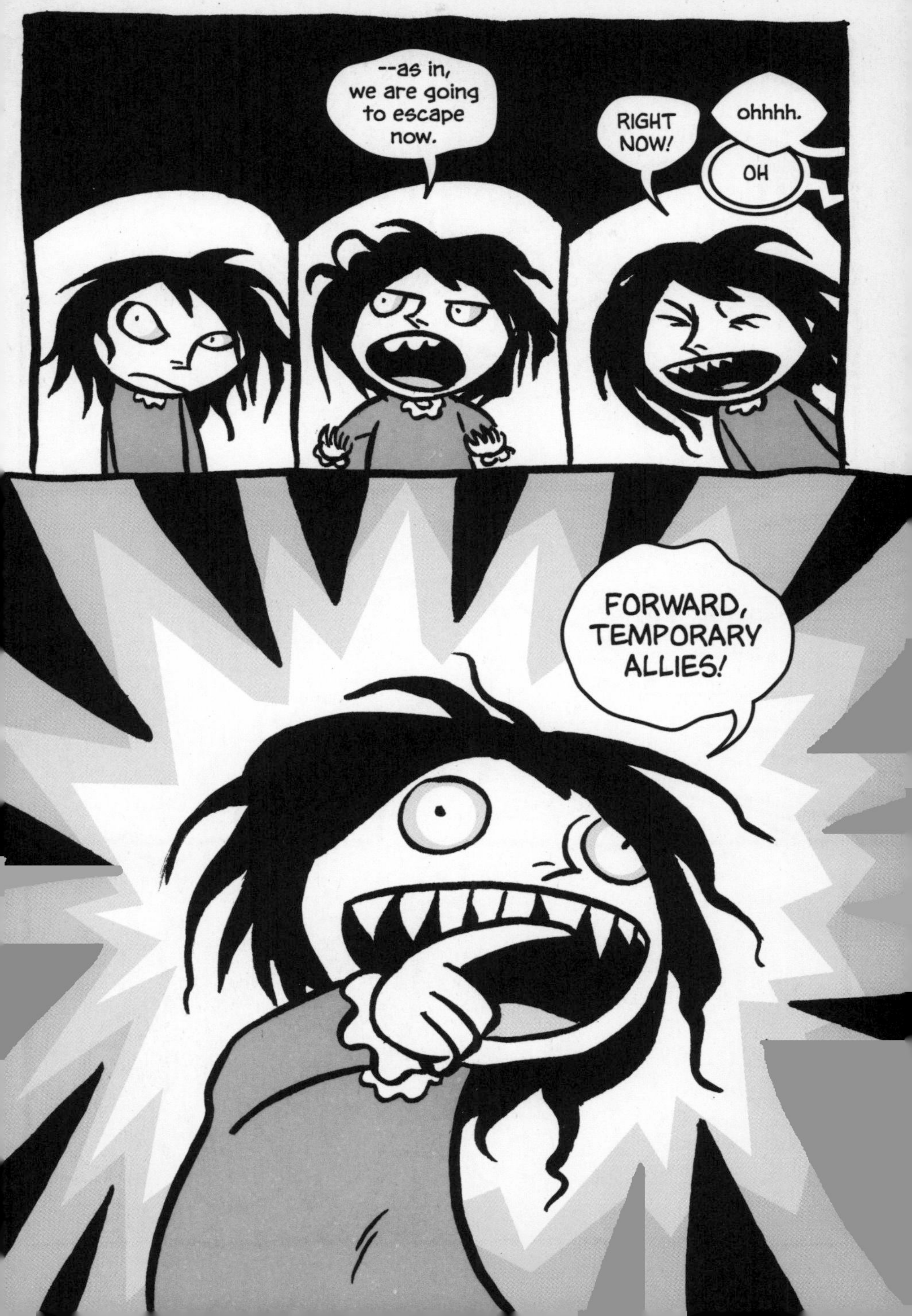
--as in, we are going to escape now.
RIGHT NOW!
ohhhh.
OH
FORWARD, TEMPORARY ALLIES!

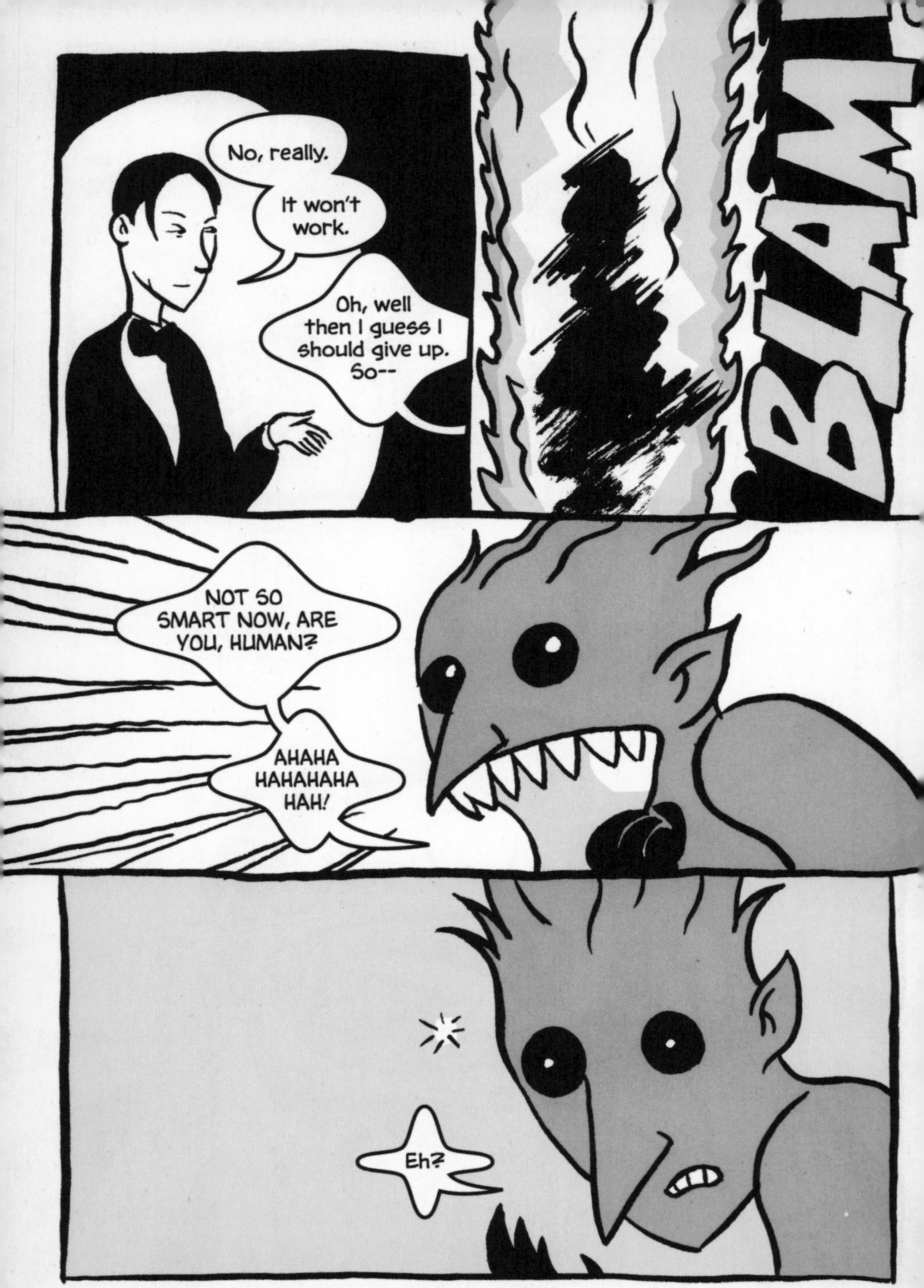

No, really.
It won't work.
Oh, well then I guess I should give up. So--
BLAM!
NOT SO SMART NOW, ARE YOU, HUMAN?
AHAHA HAHAHAHA HAH!
Eh?

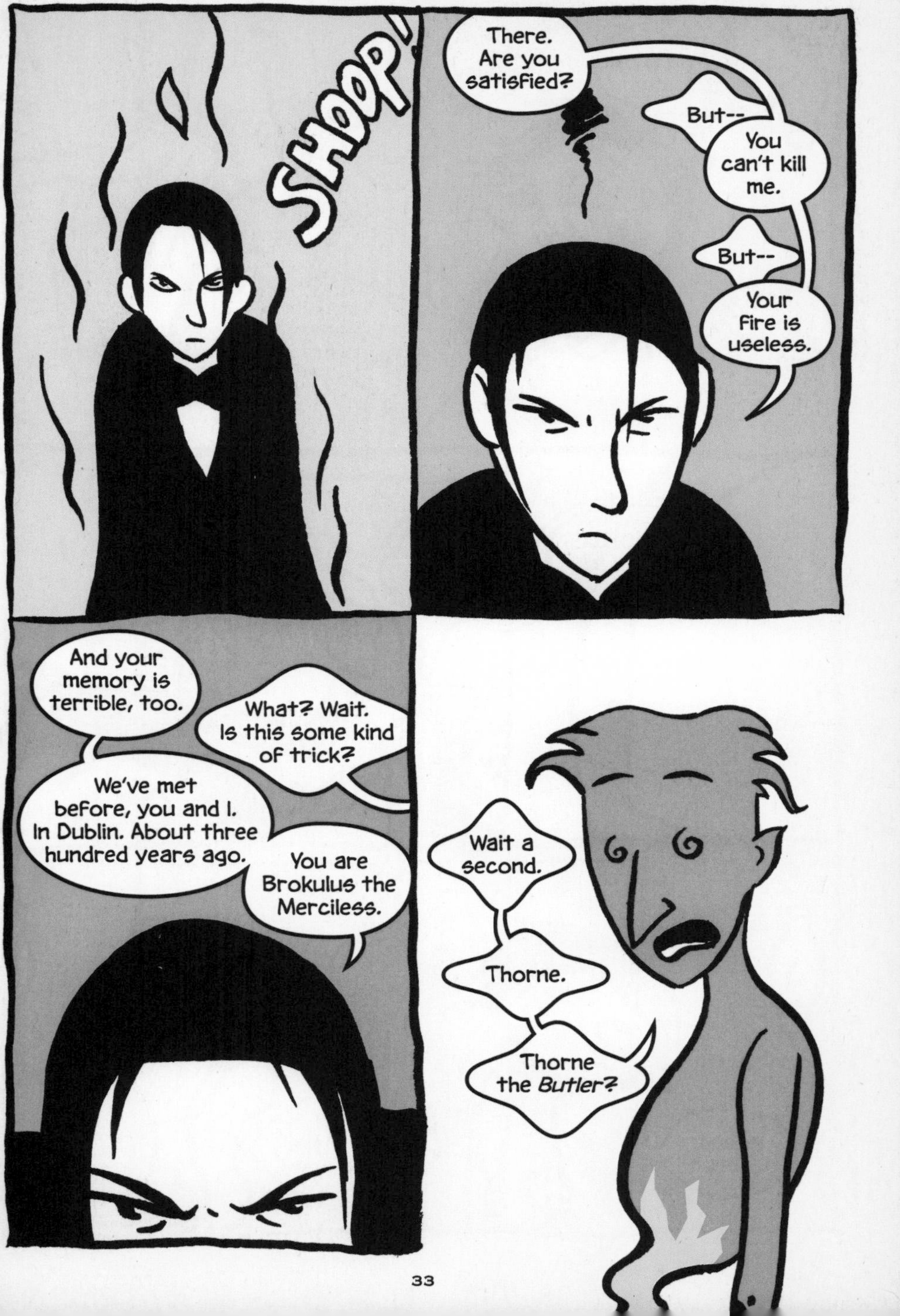
SHOOP!
There. Are you satisfied?
But--
You can't kill me.
But--
Your fire is useless.
And your memory is terrible, too.
What? Wait. Is this some kind of trick?
We've met before, you and I. In Dublin. About three hundred years ago.
You are Brokulus the Merciless.
Wait a second.
Thorne.
Thorne the *Butler*?

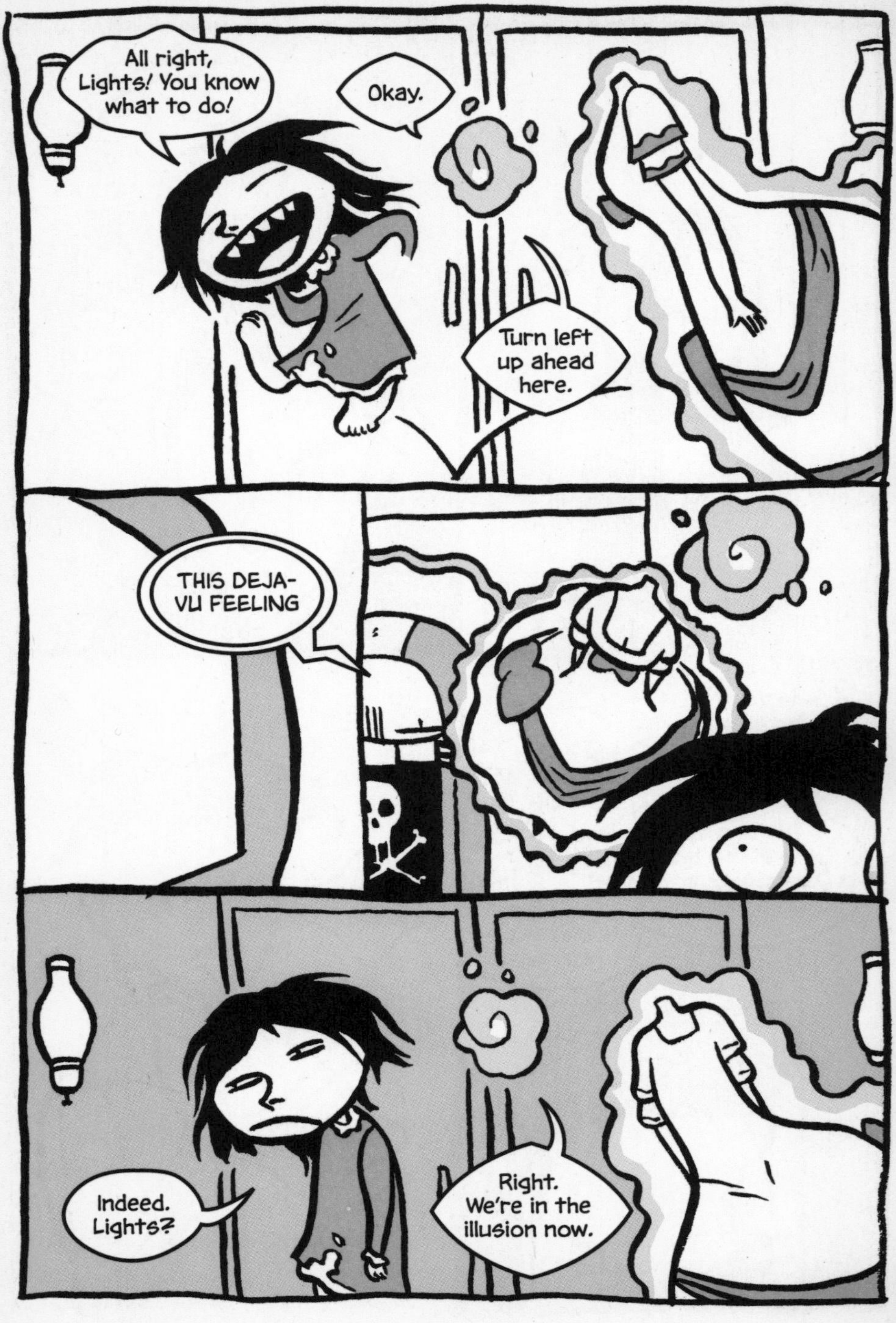
All right, Lights! You know what to do!
Okay.
Turn left up ahead here.
THIS DEJA-VU FEELING
Indeed. Lights?
Right. We're in the illusion now.

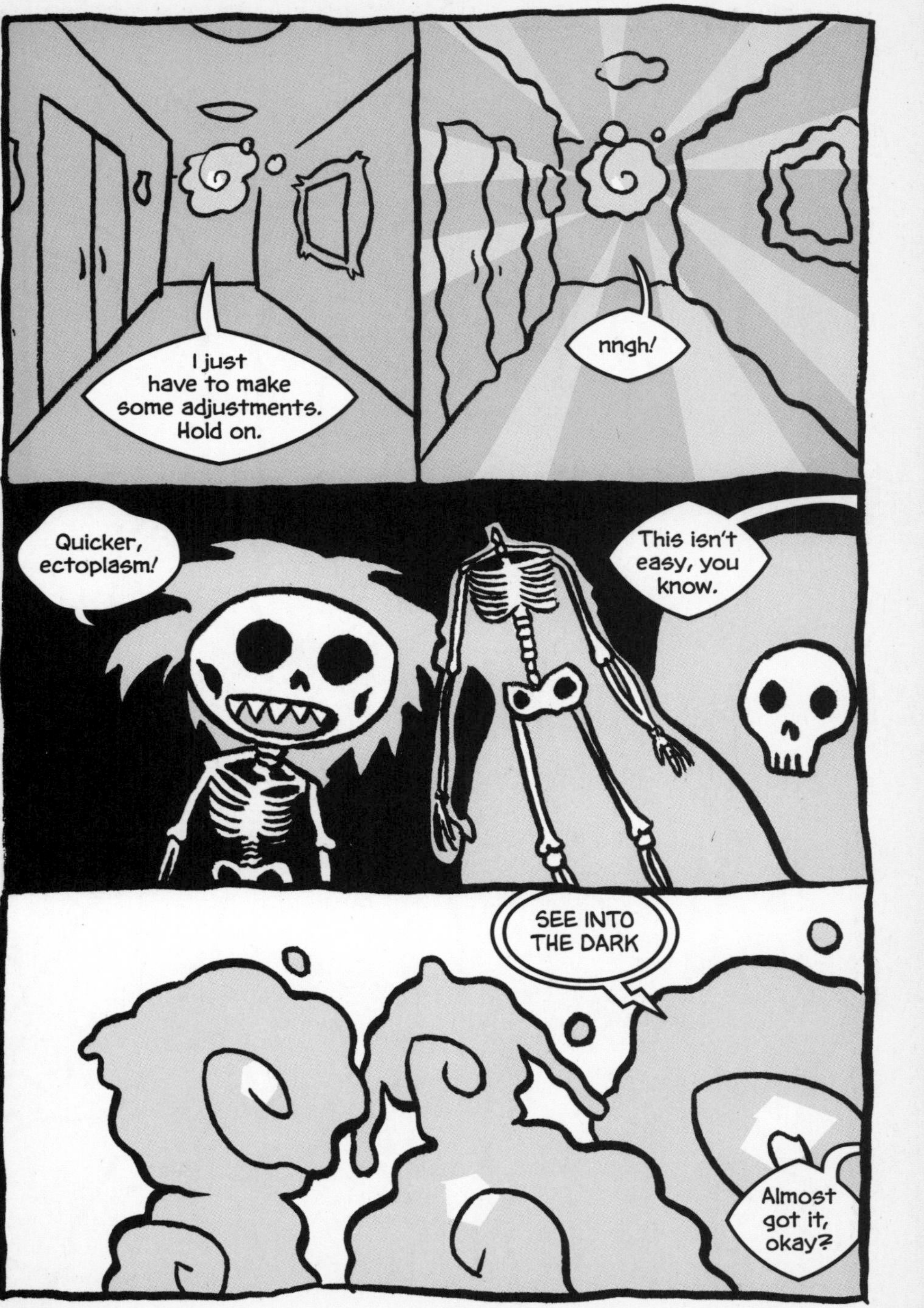
I just have to make some adjustments. Hold on.
nngh!
Quicker, ectoplasm!
This isn't easy, you know.
SEE INTO THE DARK
Almost got it, okay?

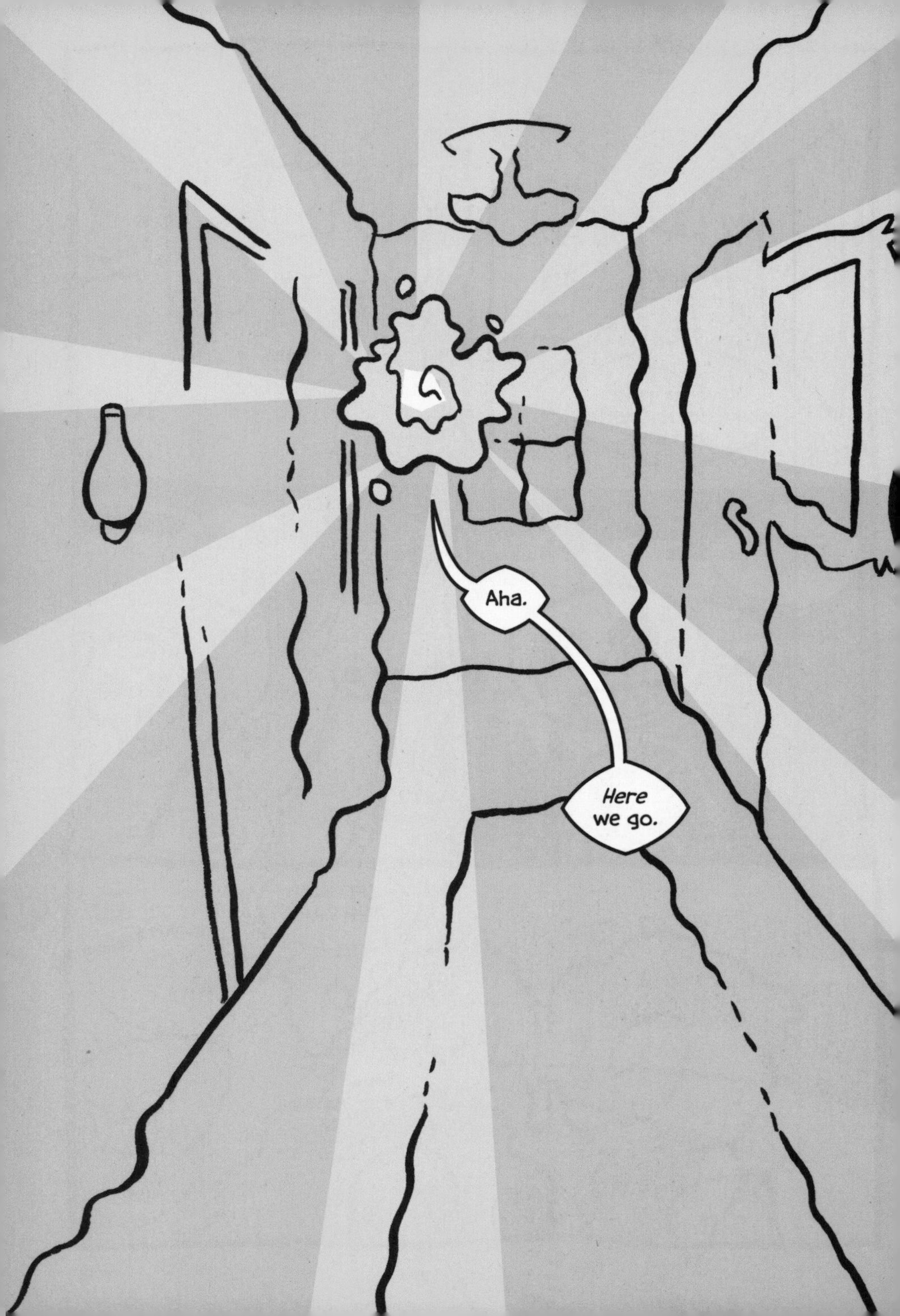
Aha.
Here we go.

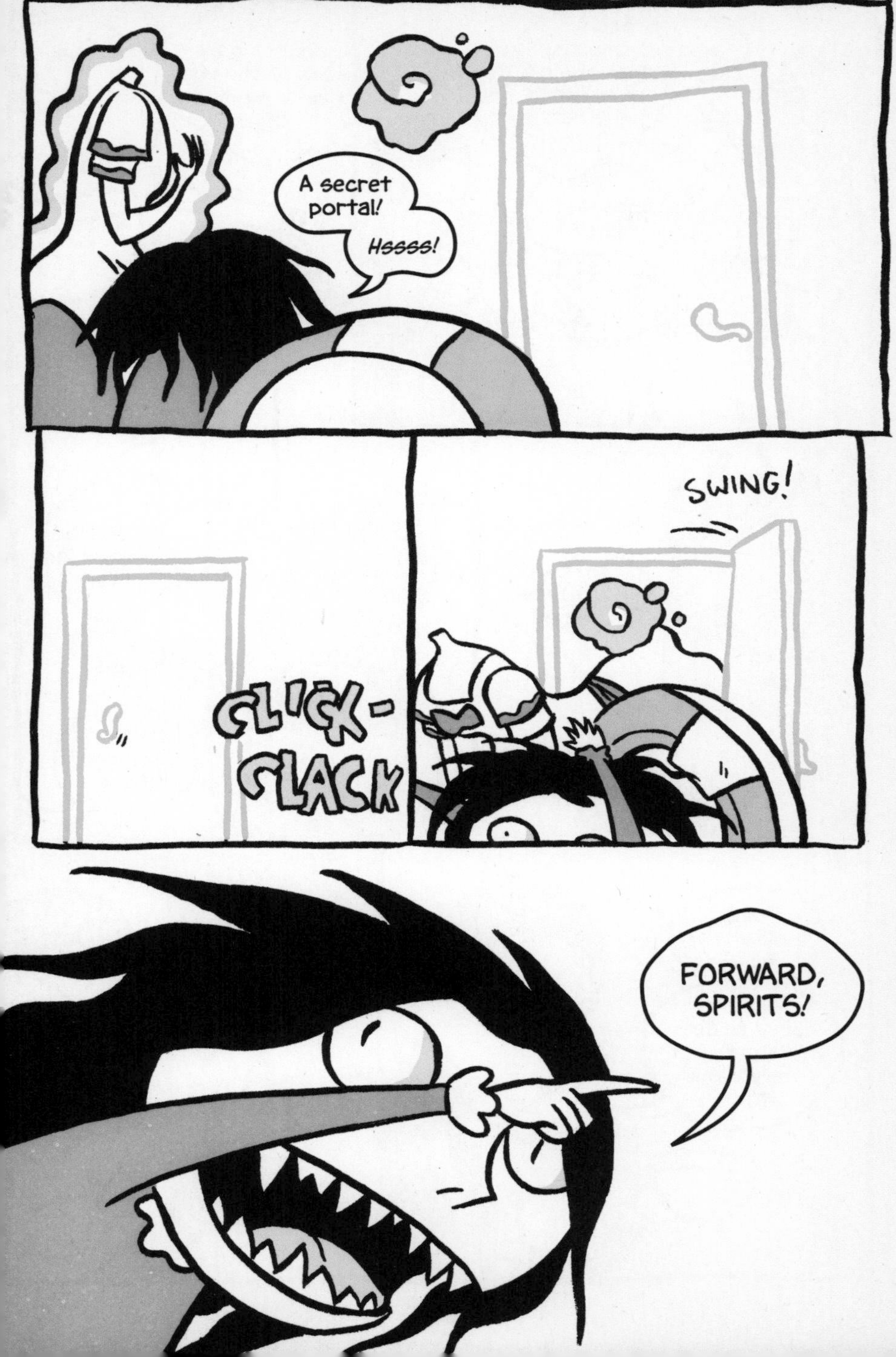
A secret portal!
Hssss!
CLICK-CLACK
SWING!
FORWARD, SPIRITS!

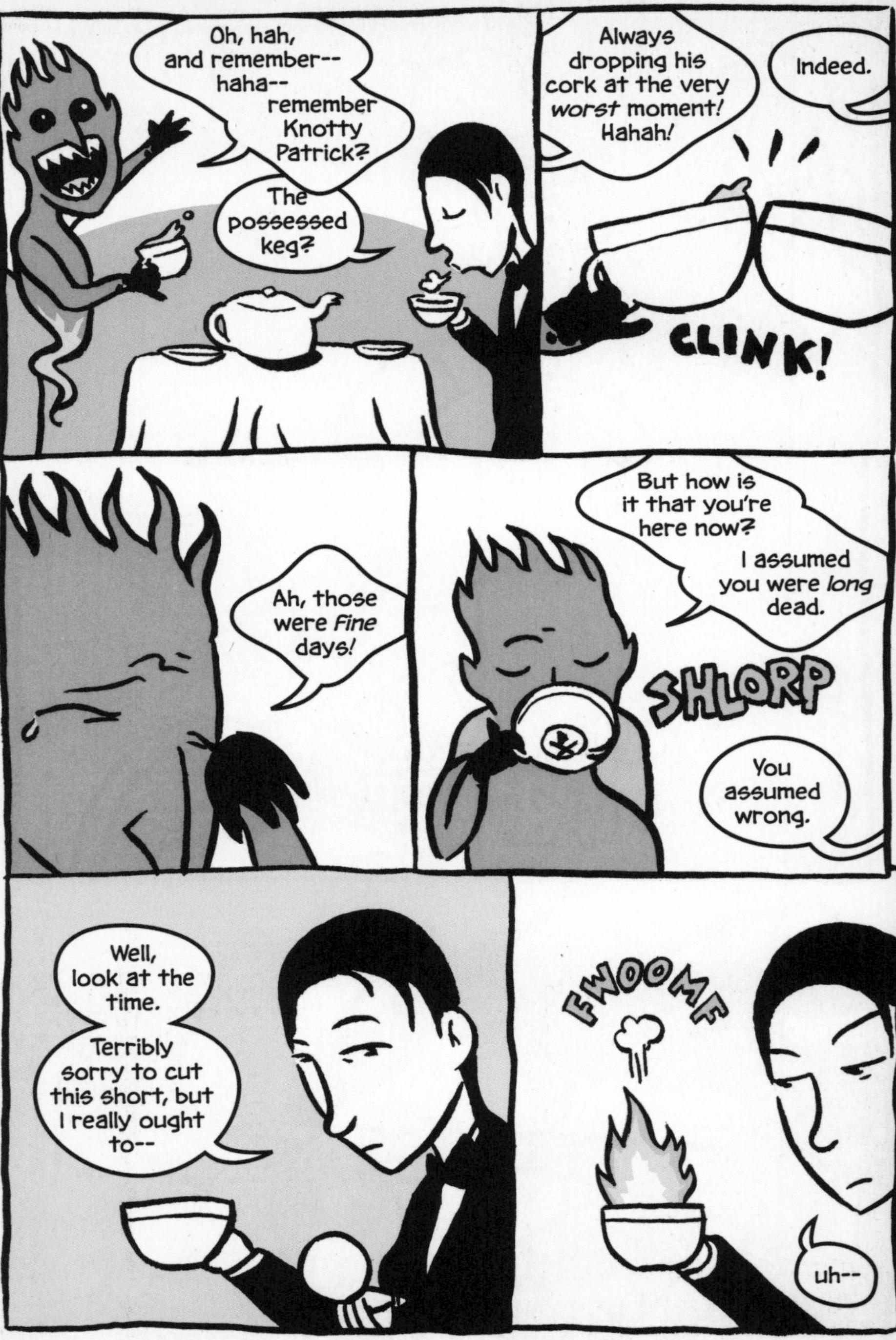
Oh, hah, and remember-- haha-- remember Knotty Patrick?
The possessed keg?
Always dropping his cork at the very *worst* moment! Hahah!
Indeed.
CLINK!
Ah, those were *fine* days!
But how is it that you're here now?
I assumed you were *long* dead.
SHLORP
You assumed wrong.
Well, look at the time.
Terribly sorry to cut this short, but I really ought to--
FWOOMF
uh--

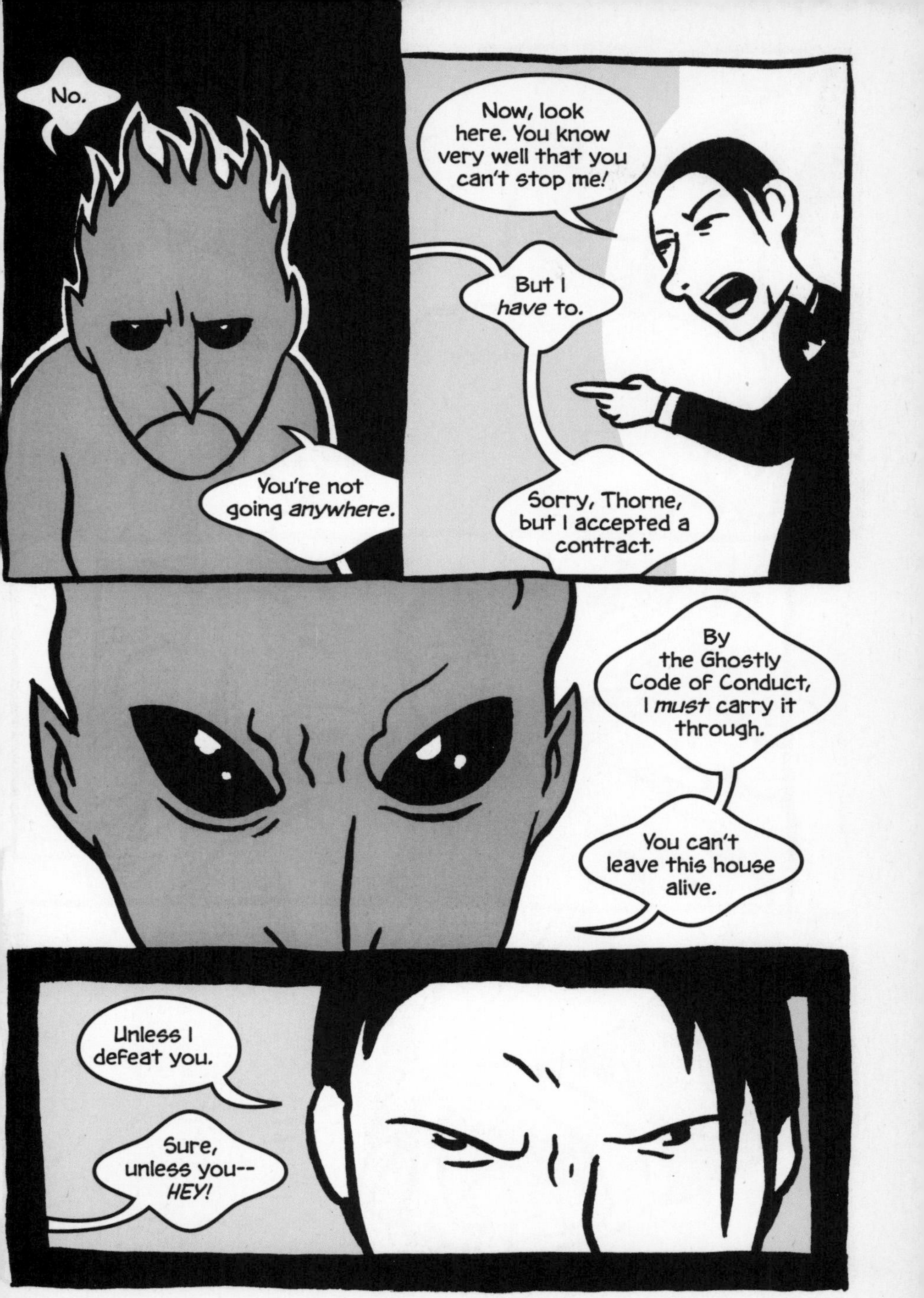
No.
You're not going *anywhere.*
Now, look here. You know very well that you can't stop me!
But I *have* to.
Sorry, Thorne, but I accepted a contract.
By the Ghostly Code of Conduct, I *must* carry it through.
You can't leave this house alive.
Unless I defeat you.
Sure, unless you-- *HEY!*

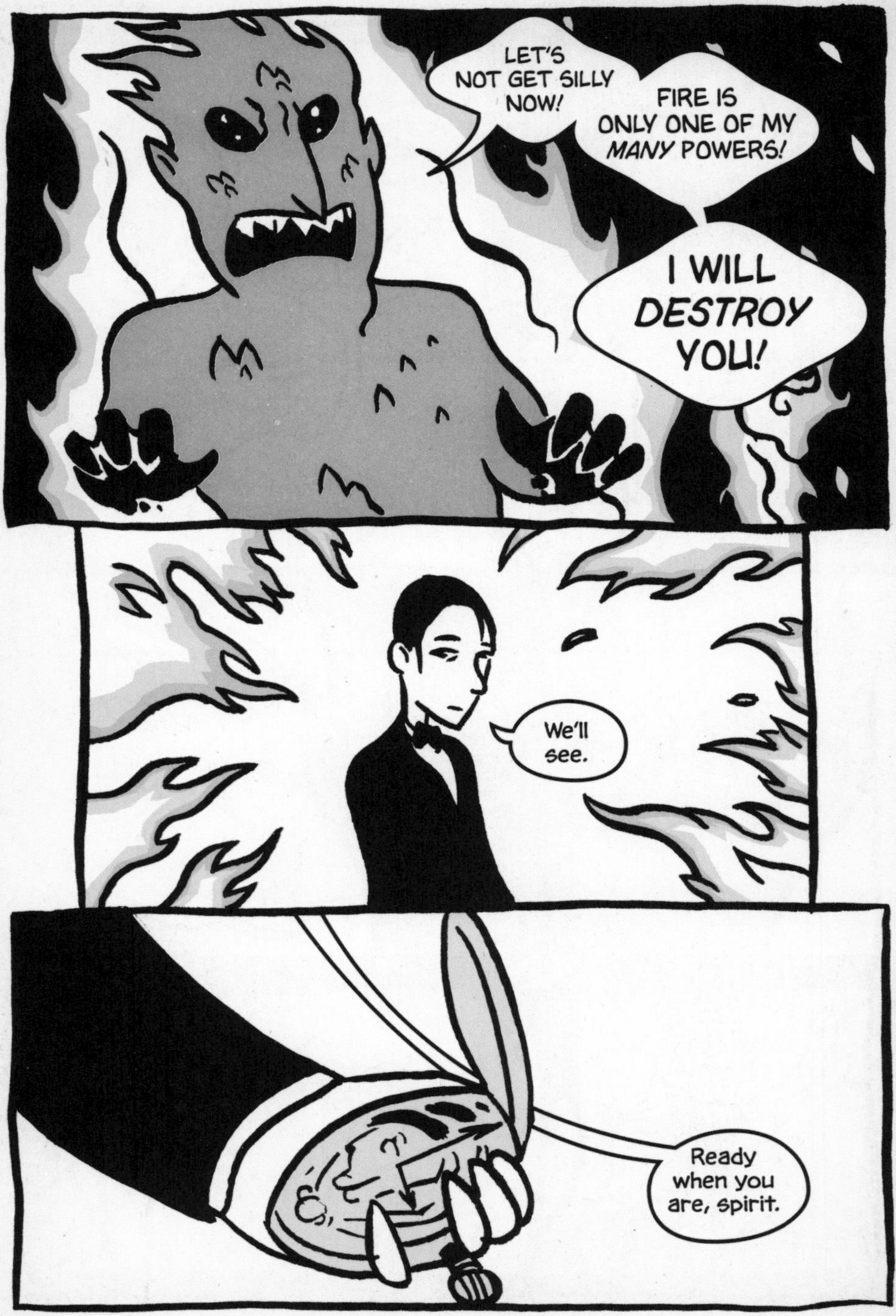
LET'S NOT GET SILLY NOW!
FIRE IS ONLY ONE OF MY *MANY* POWERS!
I WILL *DESTROY* YOU!
We'll see.
Ready when you are, spirit.

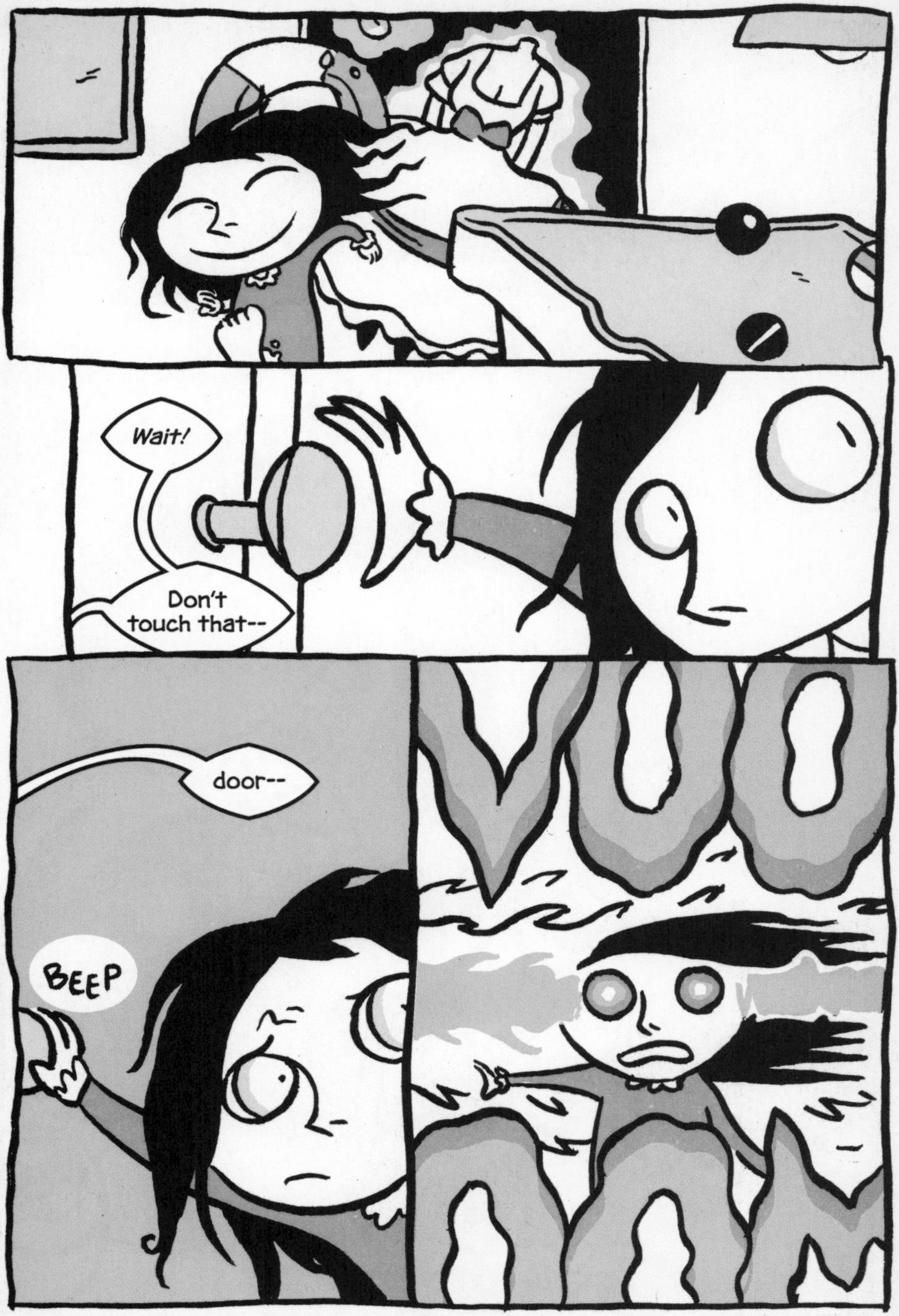
Wait!
Don't touch that--
door--
BEEP
VOOOM

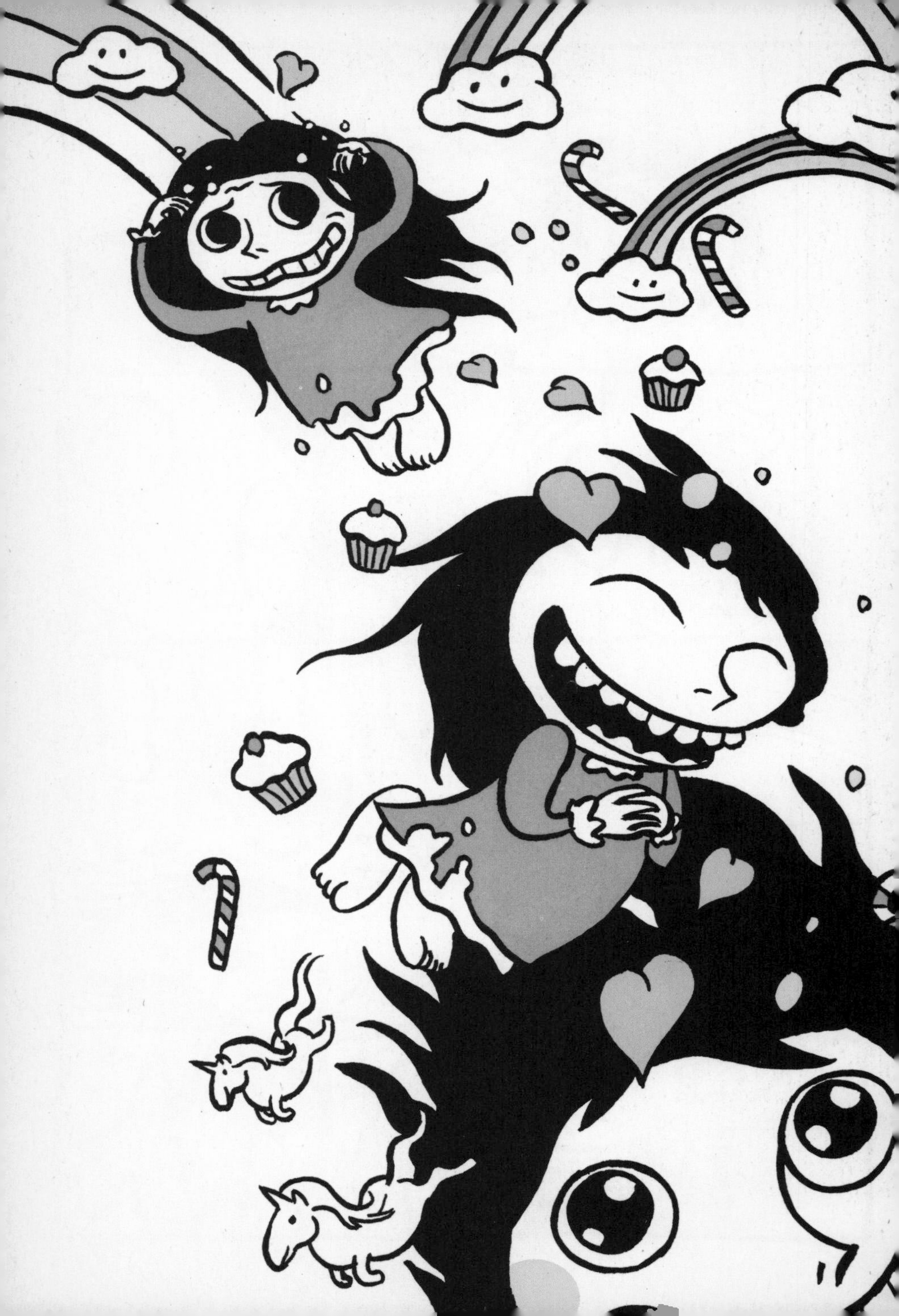

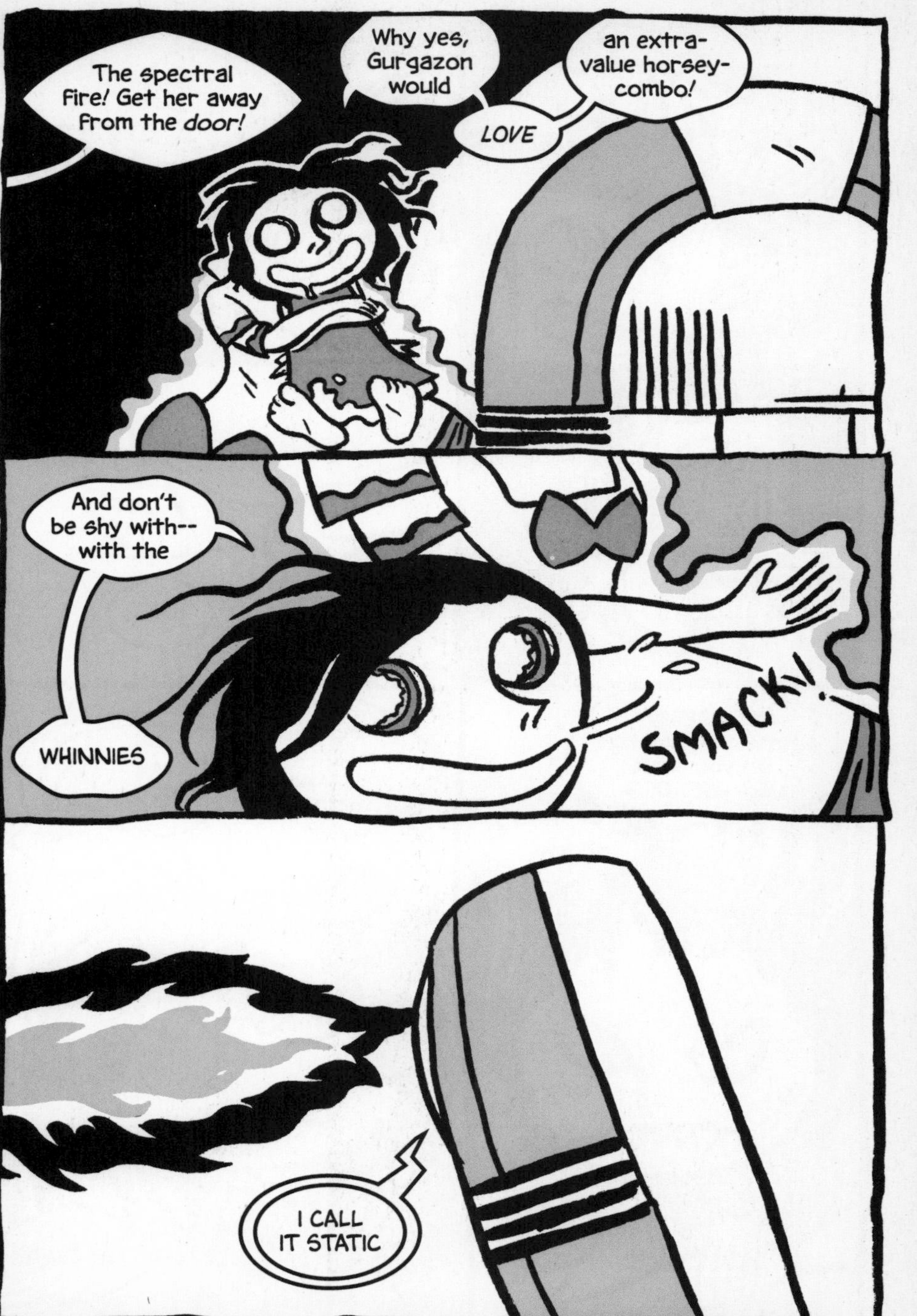
The spectral fire! Get her away from the *door!*
Why yes, Gurgazon would
LOVE
an extra-value horsey-combo!
And don't be shy with--with the
WHINNIES
SMACK!!
I CALL IT STATIC

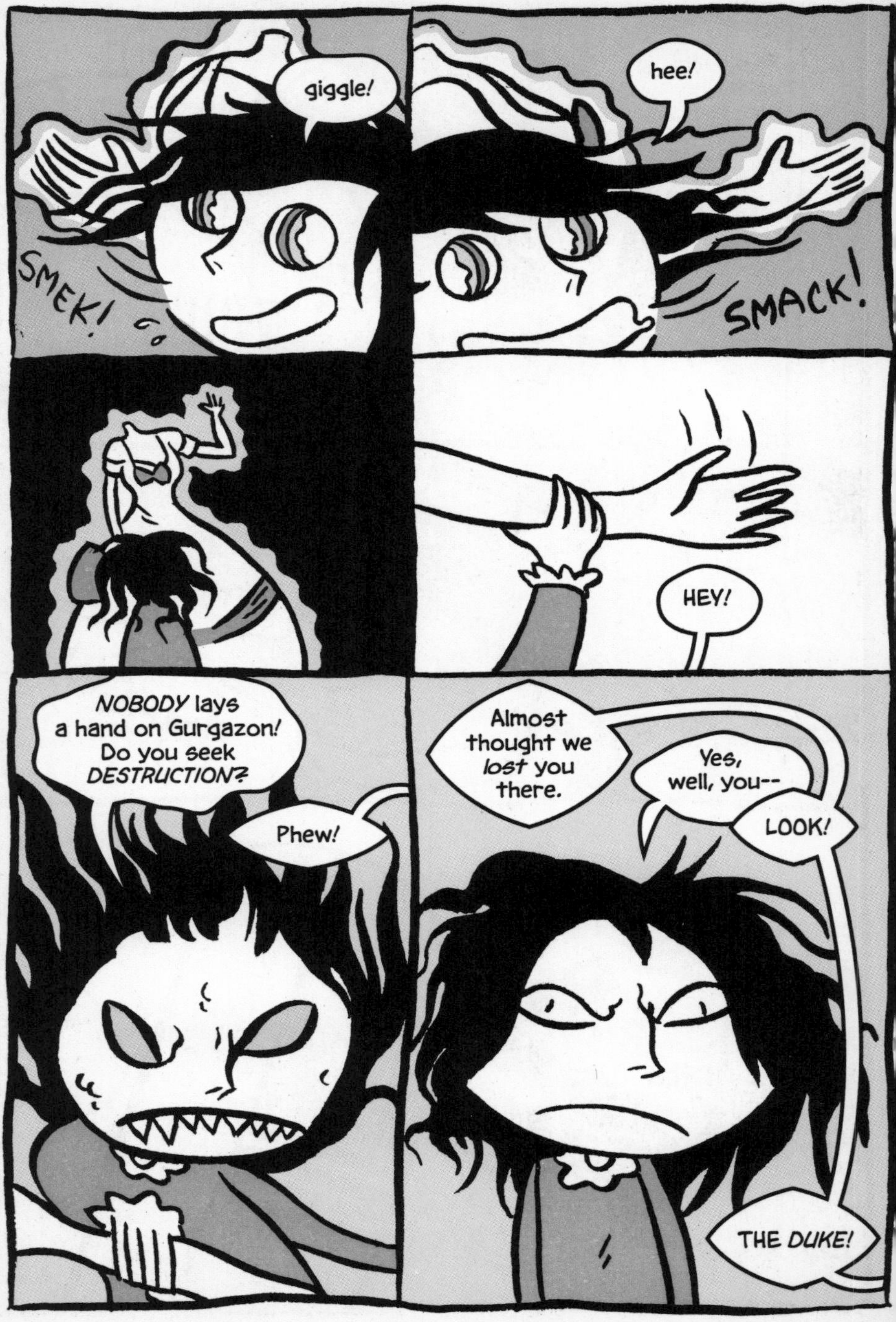
giggle!
SMEK!
hee!
SMACK!
HEY!
NOBODY lays a hand on Gurgazon! Do you seek *DESTRUCTION*?
Phew!
Almost thought we *lost* you there.
Yes, well, you--
LOOK!
THE *DUKE*!

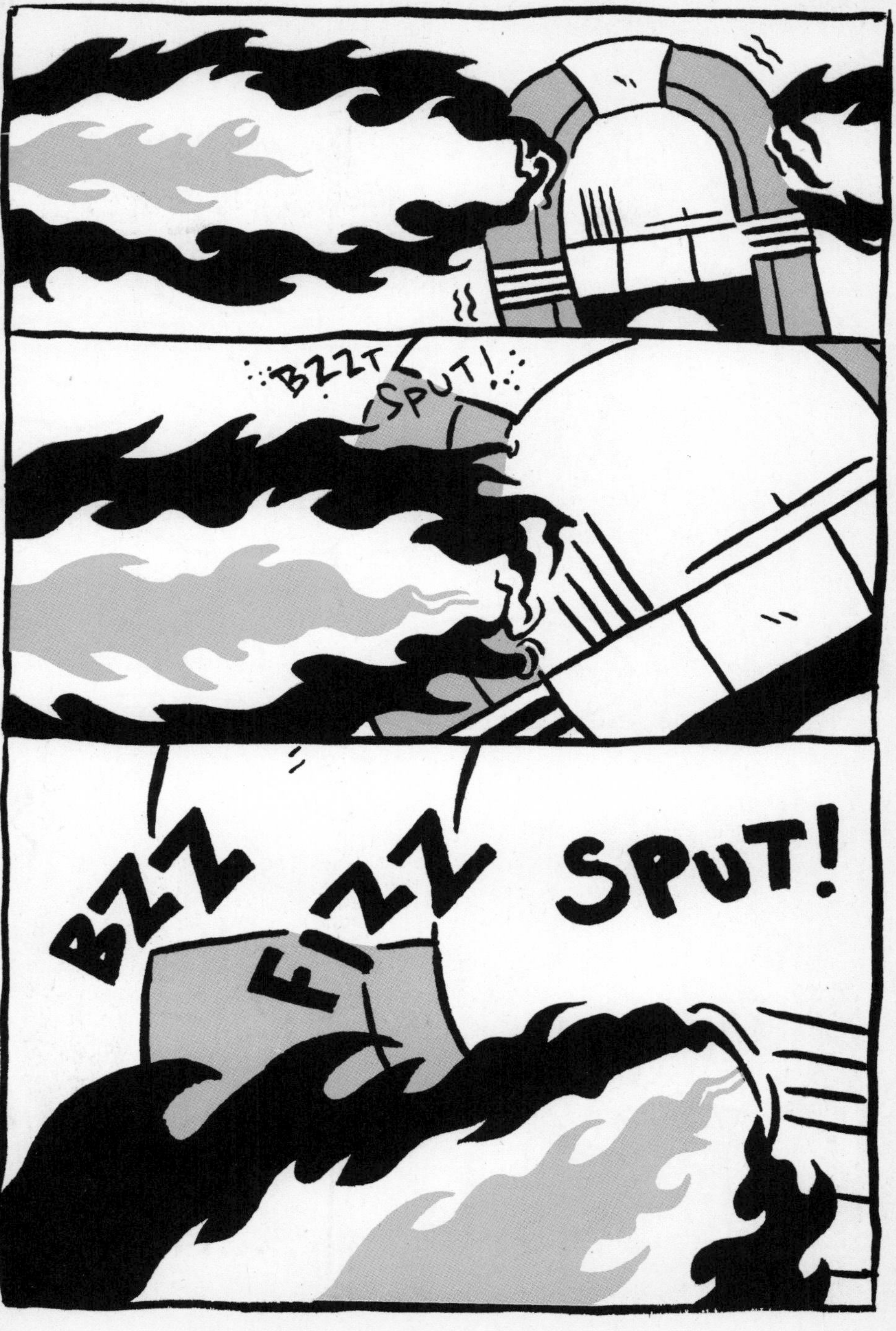
BZZT
SPUT!
BZZ
FIZZ
SPUT!

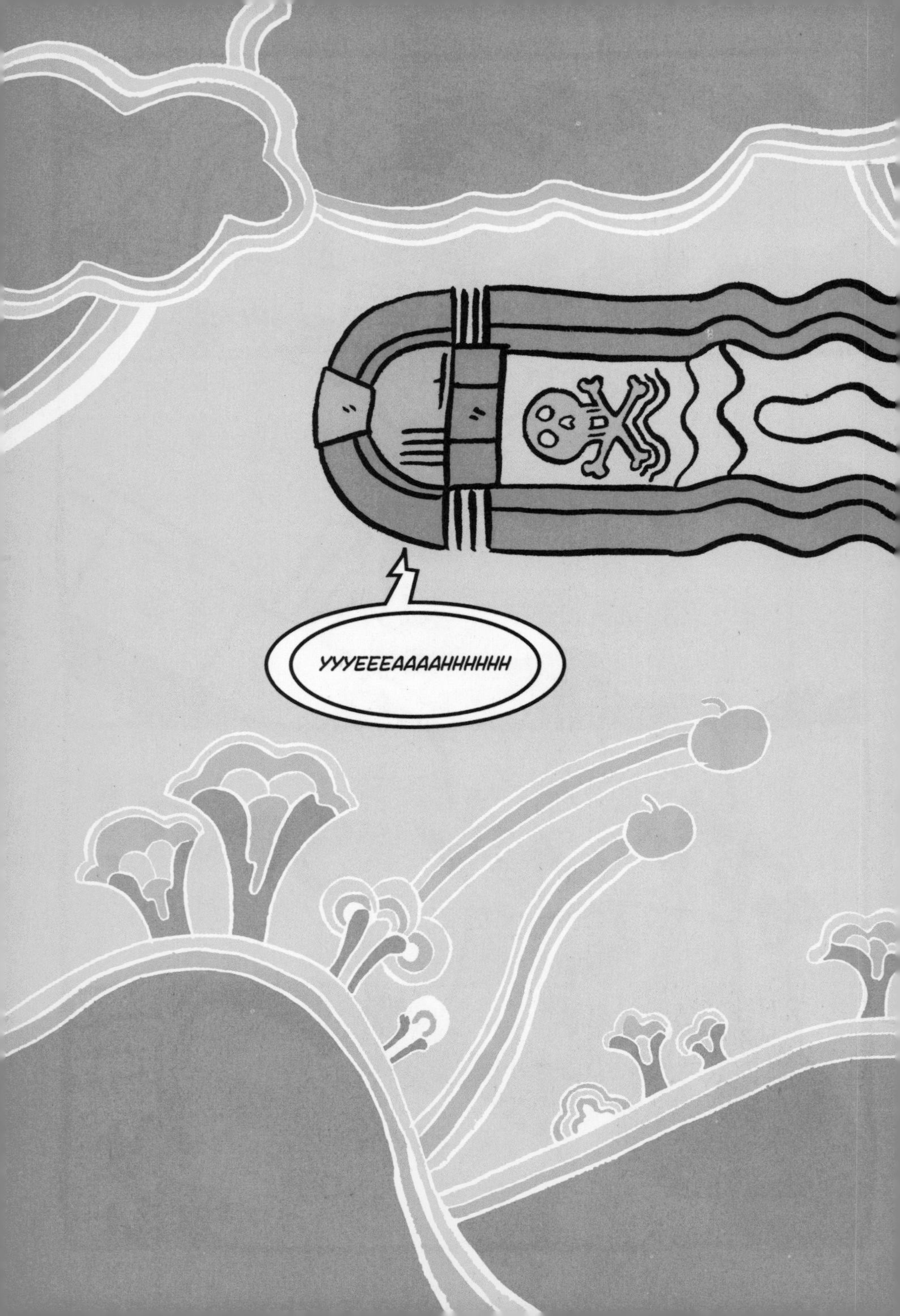
YYYEEEAAAAHHHHHH

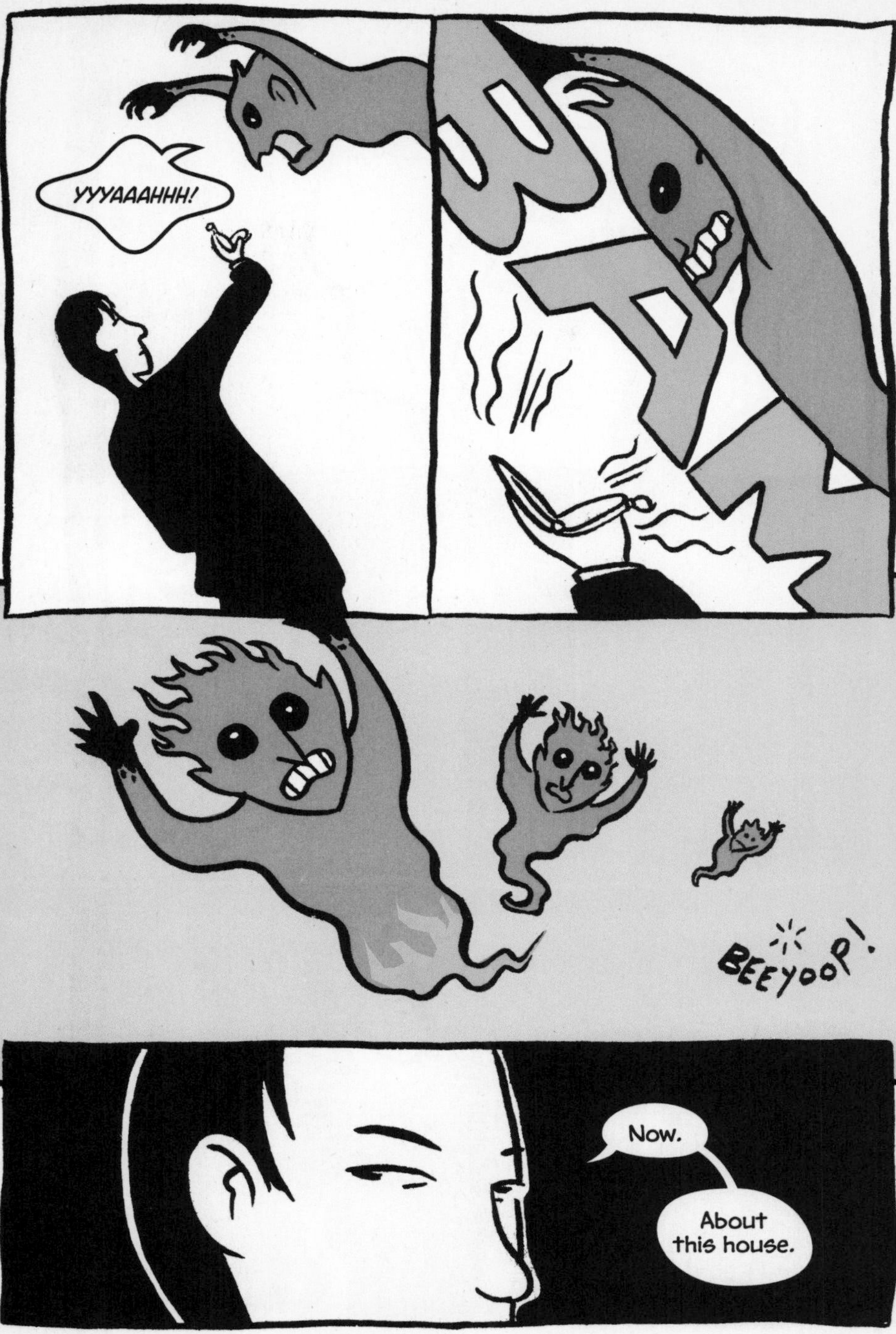
YYYAAAHHH!
BEEYOOP!
Now.
About this house.

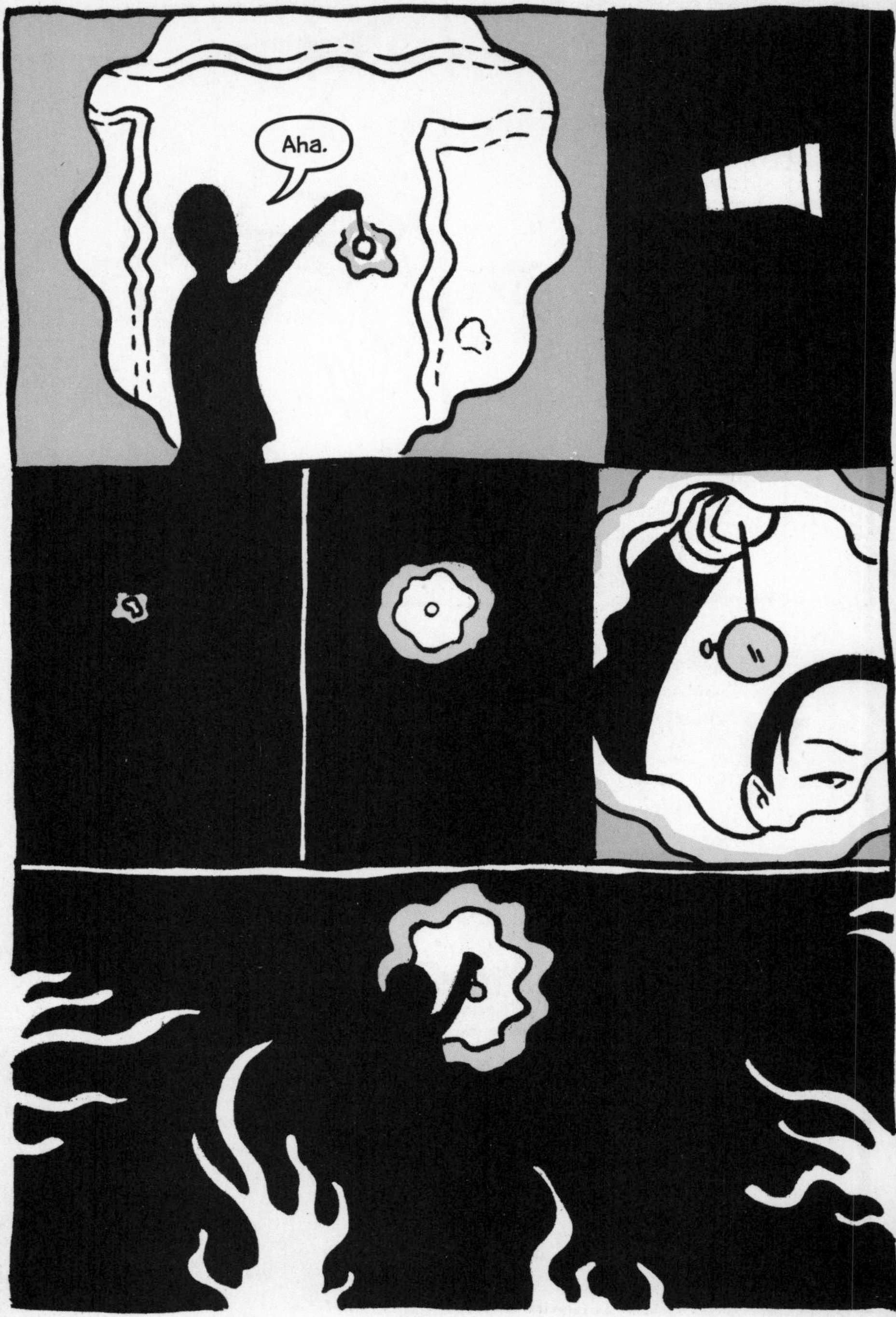
Aha.

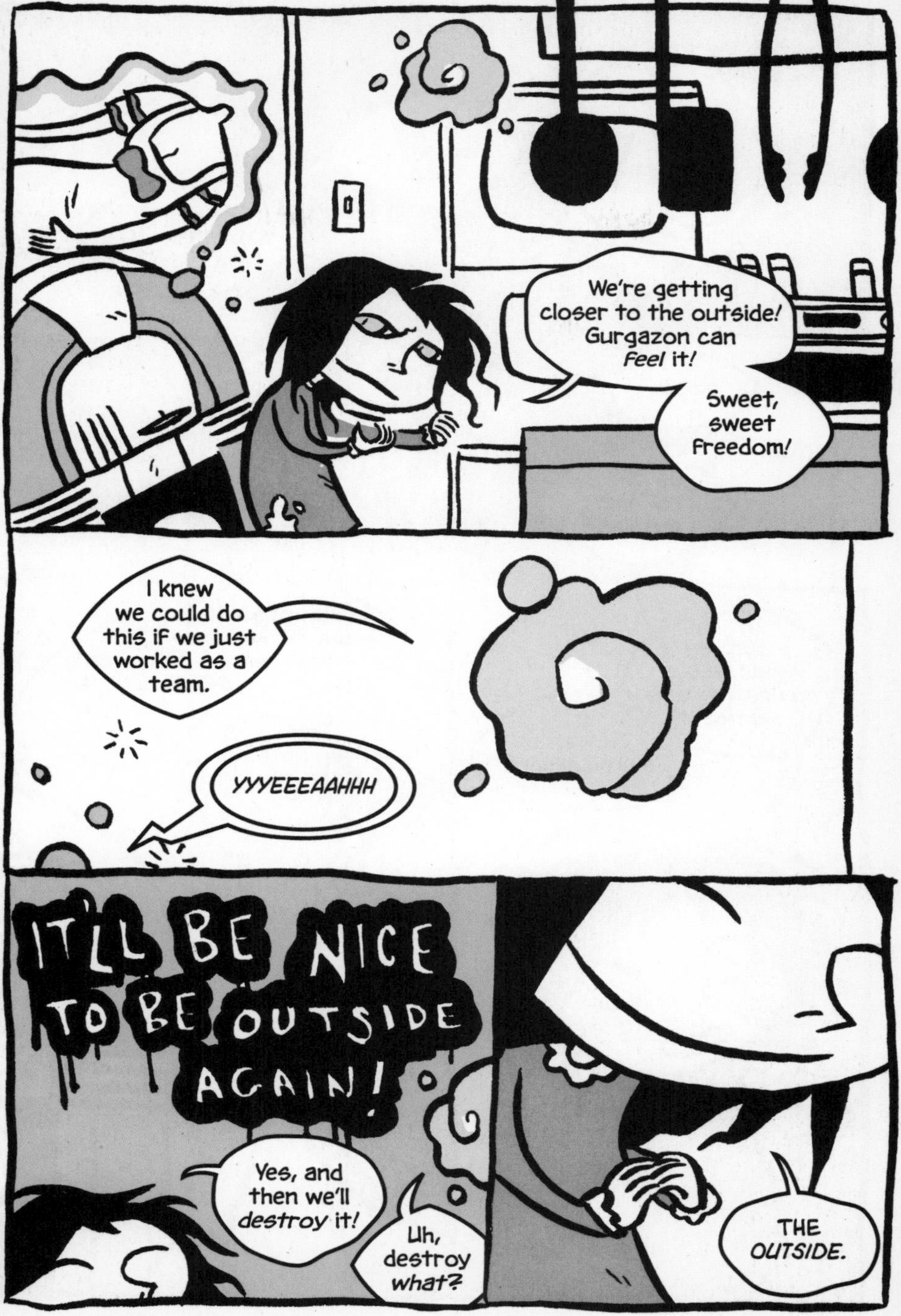

We're getting closer to the outside! Gurgazon can *feel* it!
Sweet, sweet freedom!
I knew we could do this if we just worked as a team.
YYYEEEAAHHH
IT'LL BE NICE TO BE OUTSIDE AGAIN!
Yes, and then we'll *destroy* it!
Uh, destroy *what?*
THE *OUTSIDE.*

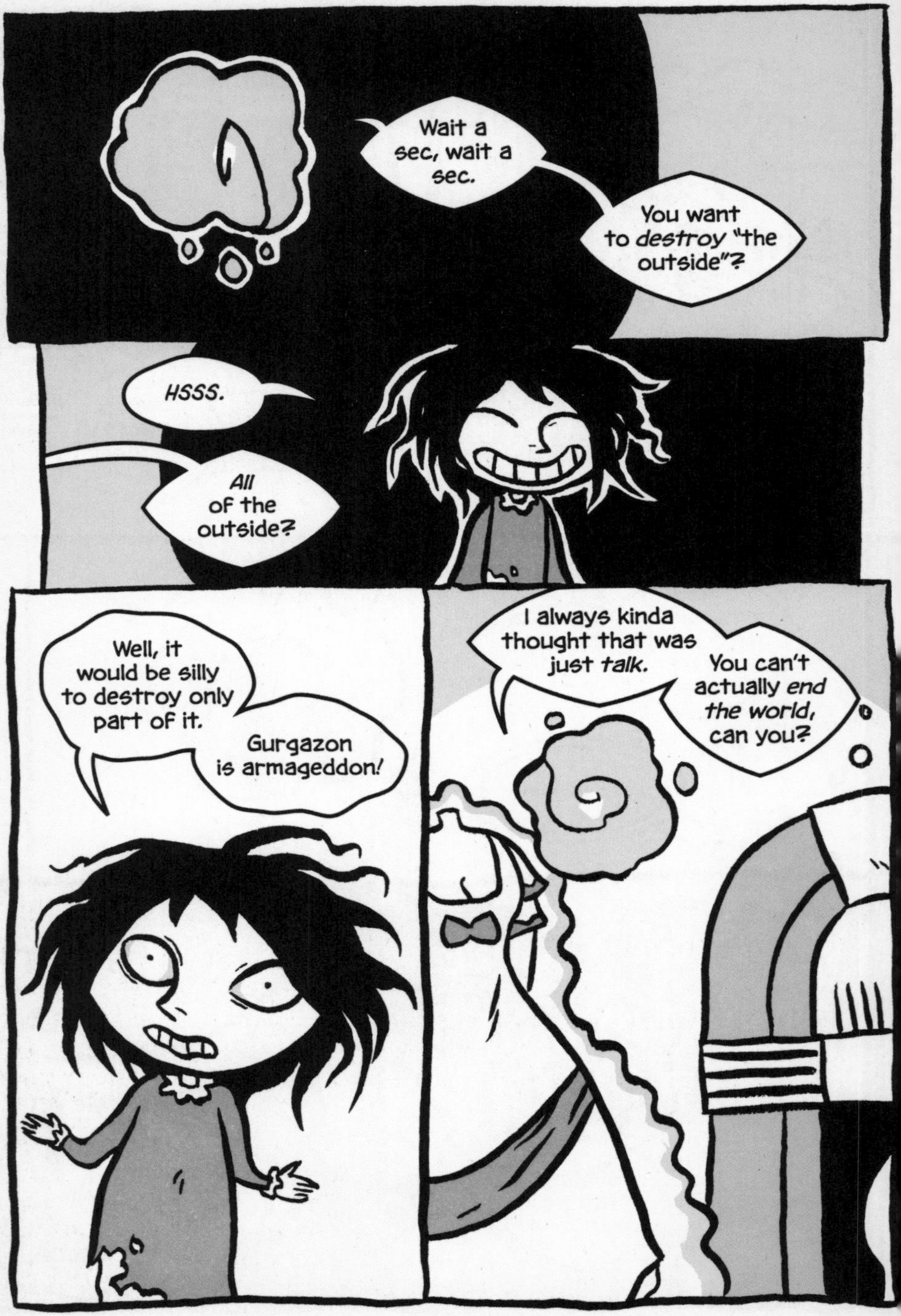

Wait a sec, wait a sec.
You want to *destroy* "the outside"?
HSSS.
All of the outside?
Well, it would be silly to destroy only part of it.
Gurgazon is armageddon!
I always kinda thought that was just *talk.*
You can't actually *end the world,* can you?

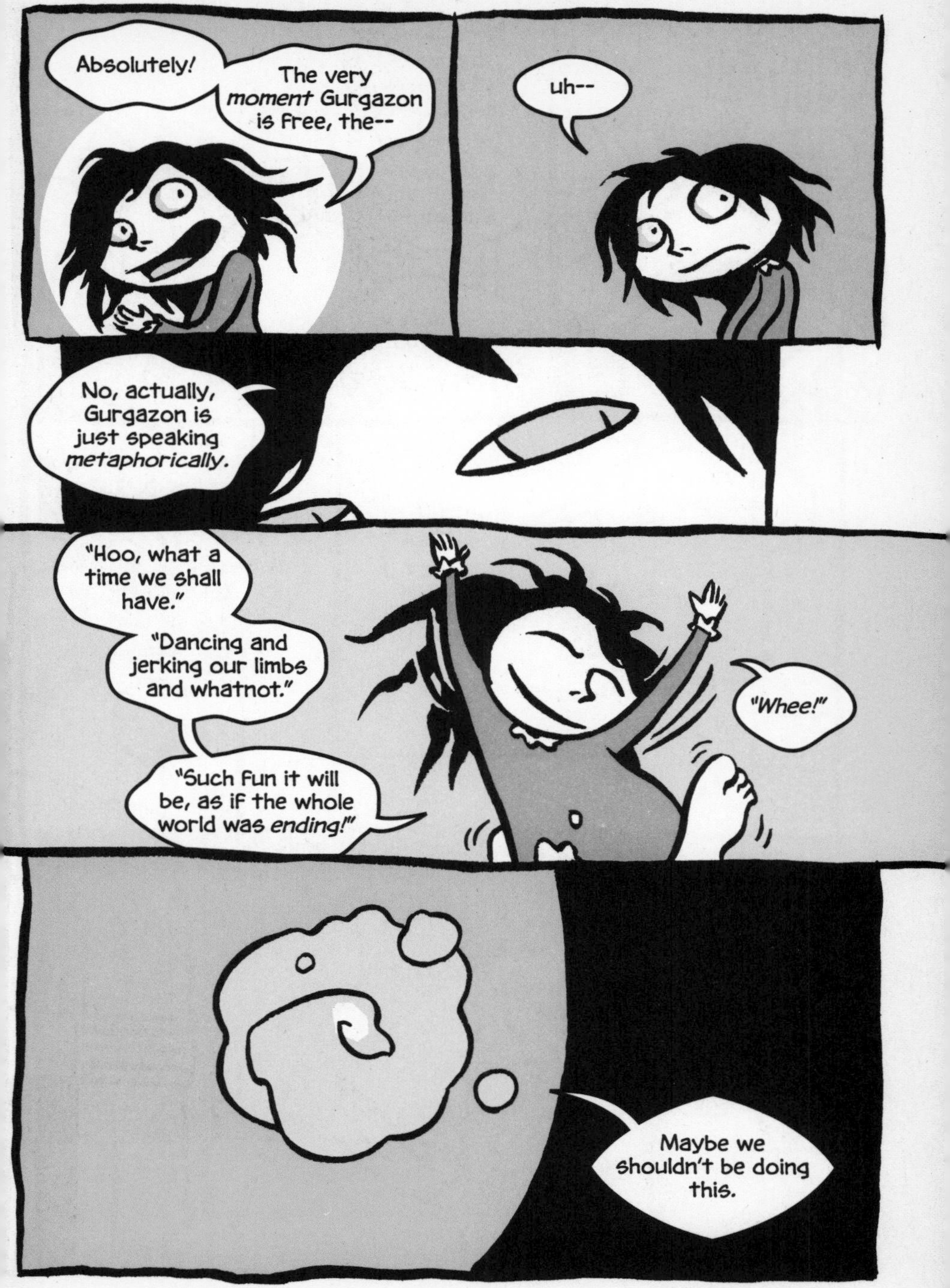
Absolutely!
The very *moment* Gurgazon is free, the--
uh--
No, actually, Gurgazon is just speaking *metaphorically*.
"Hoo, what a time we shall have."
"Dancing and jerking our limbs and whatnot."
"Such fun it will be, as if the whole world was *ending!*"
"Whee!"
Maybe we shouldn't be doing this.

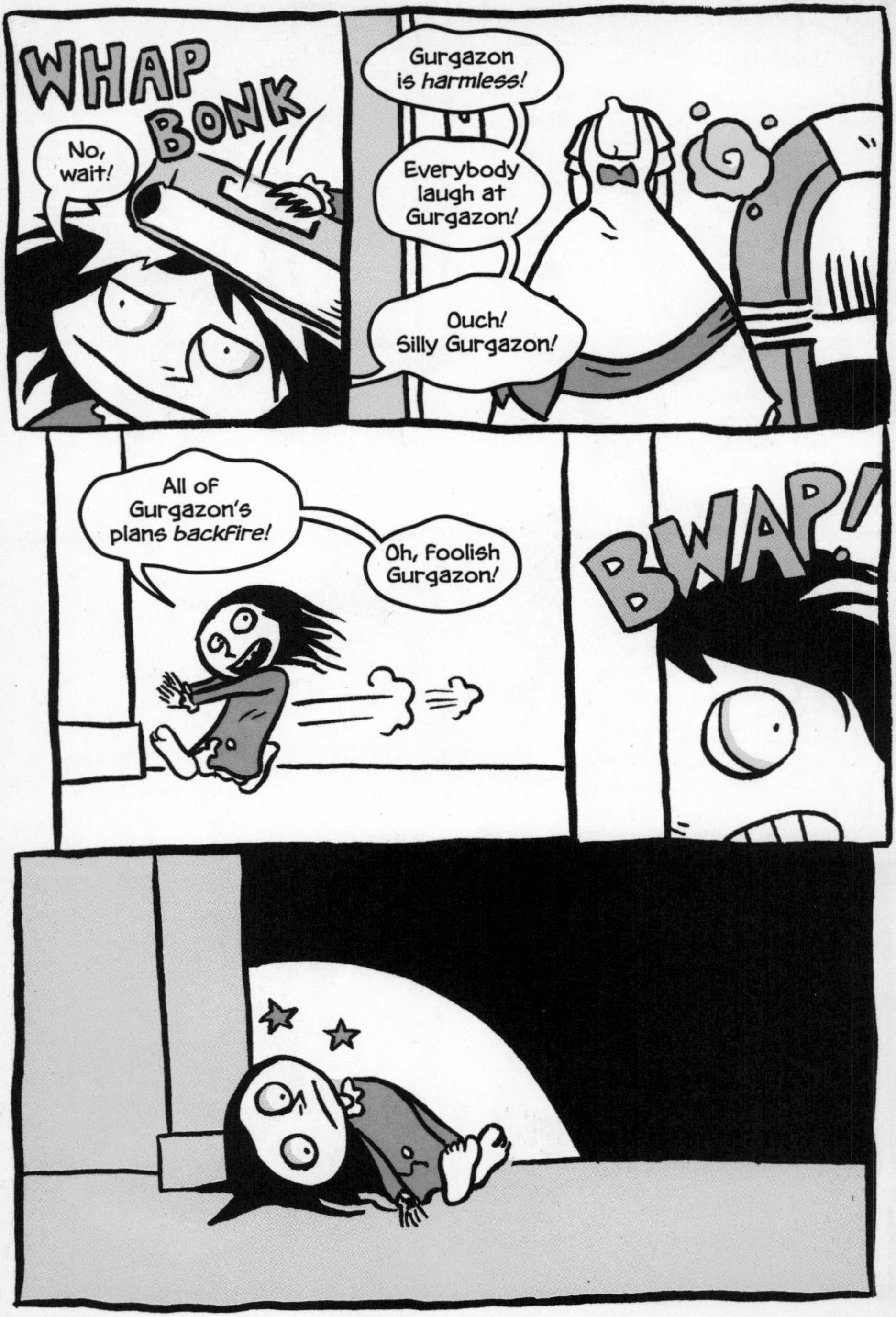
WHAP
BONK
No, wait!
Gurgazon is *harmless!*
Everybody laugh at Gurgazon!
Ouch! Silly Gurgazon!
All of Gurgazon's plans *backfire!*
Oh, foolish Gurgazon!
BWAP!

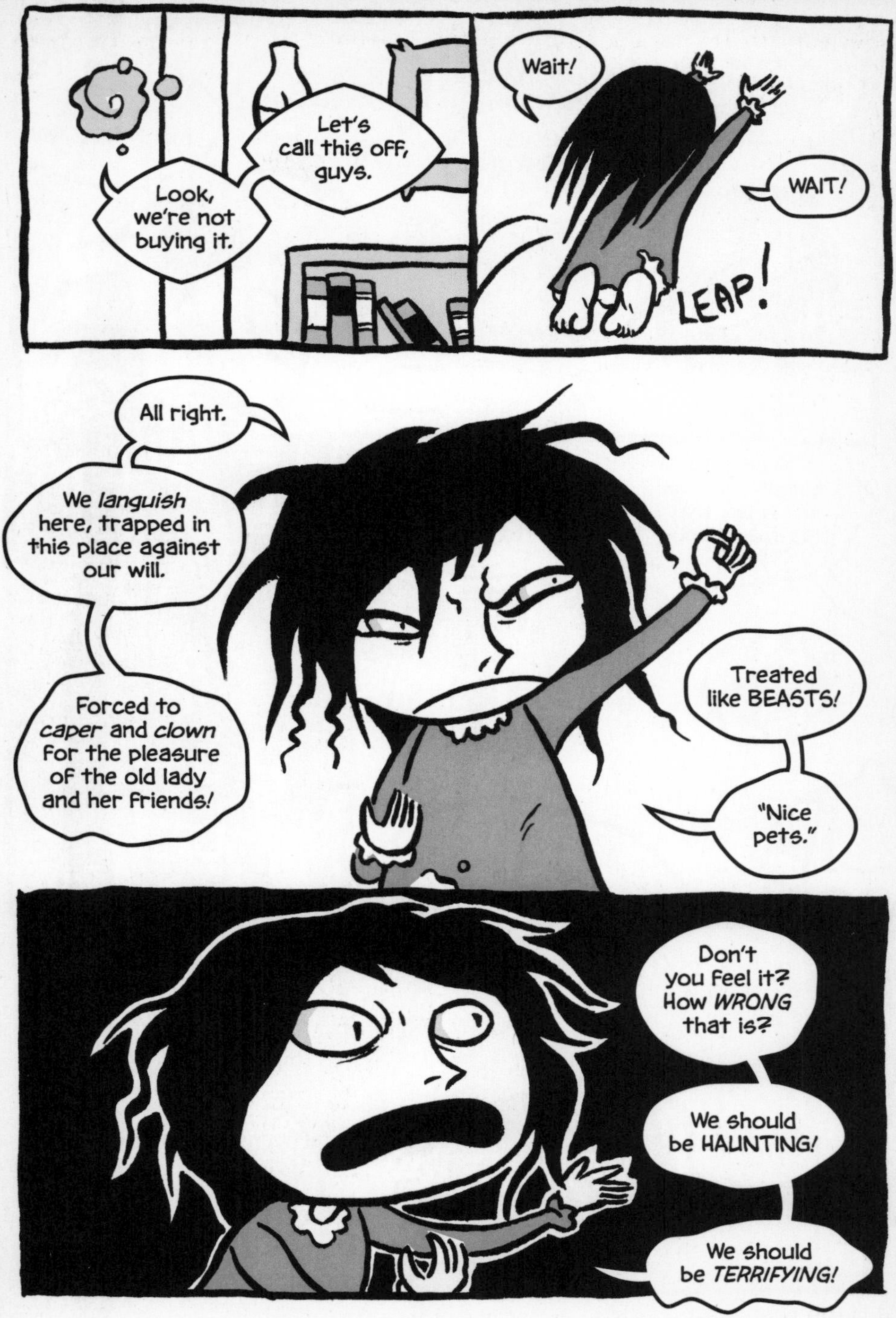
Look, we're not buying it.
Let's call this off, guys.
Wait!
WAIT!
LEAP!
All right.
We *languish* here, trapped in this place against our will.
Forced to *caper* and *clown* for the pleasure of the old lady and her friends!
Treated like BEASTS!
"Nice pets."
Don't you feel it? How *WRONG* that is?
We should be HAUNTING!
We should be *TERRIFYING!*

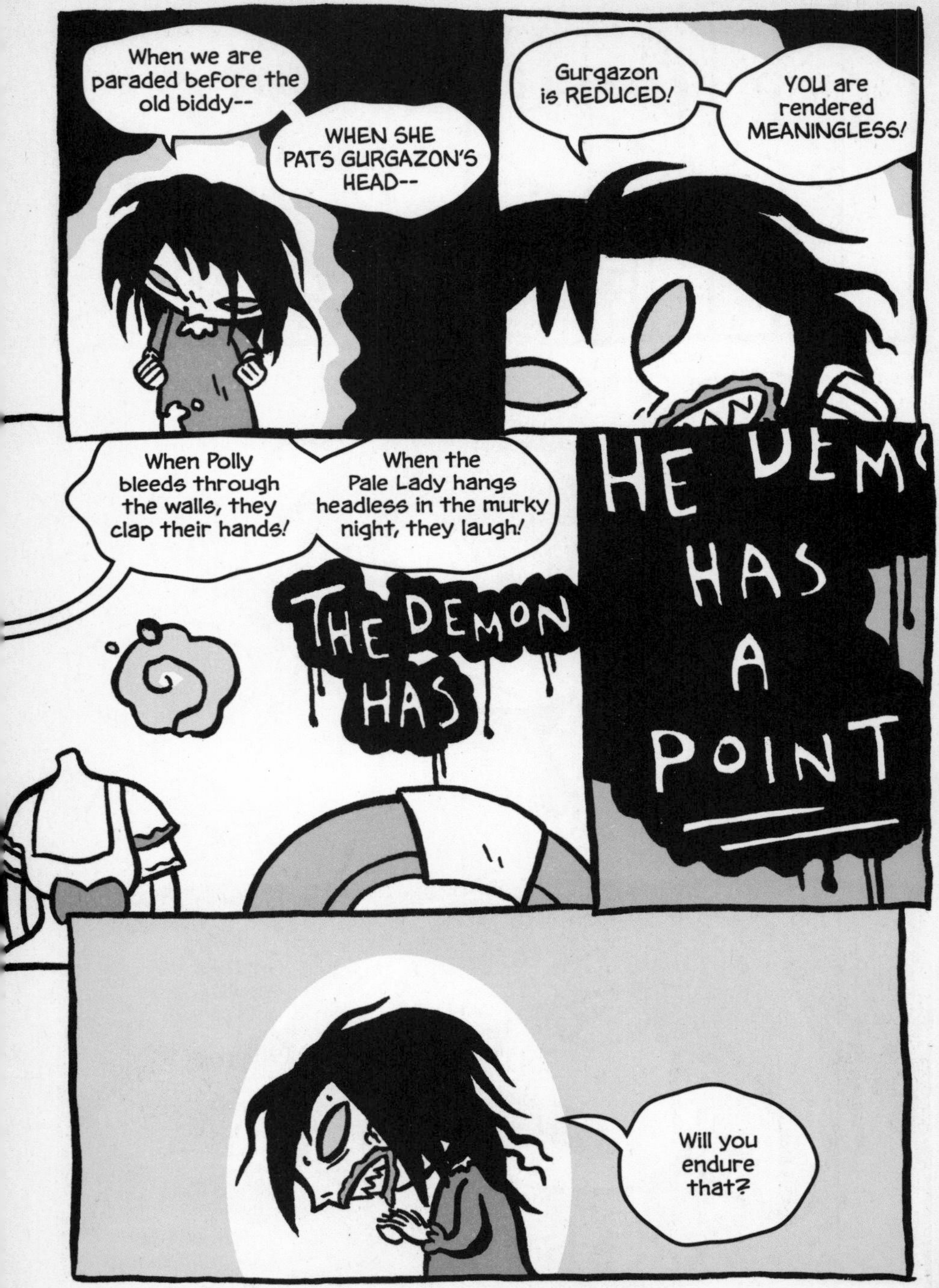
When we are paraded before the old biddy--
WHEN SHE PATS GURGAZON'S HEAD--
Gurgazon is REDUCED!
YOU are rendered MEANINGLESS!
When Polly bleeds through the walls, they clap their hands!
When the Pale Lady hangs headless in the murky night, they laugh!
THE DEMON HAS
HE DEMO HAS A POINT
Will you endure that?

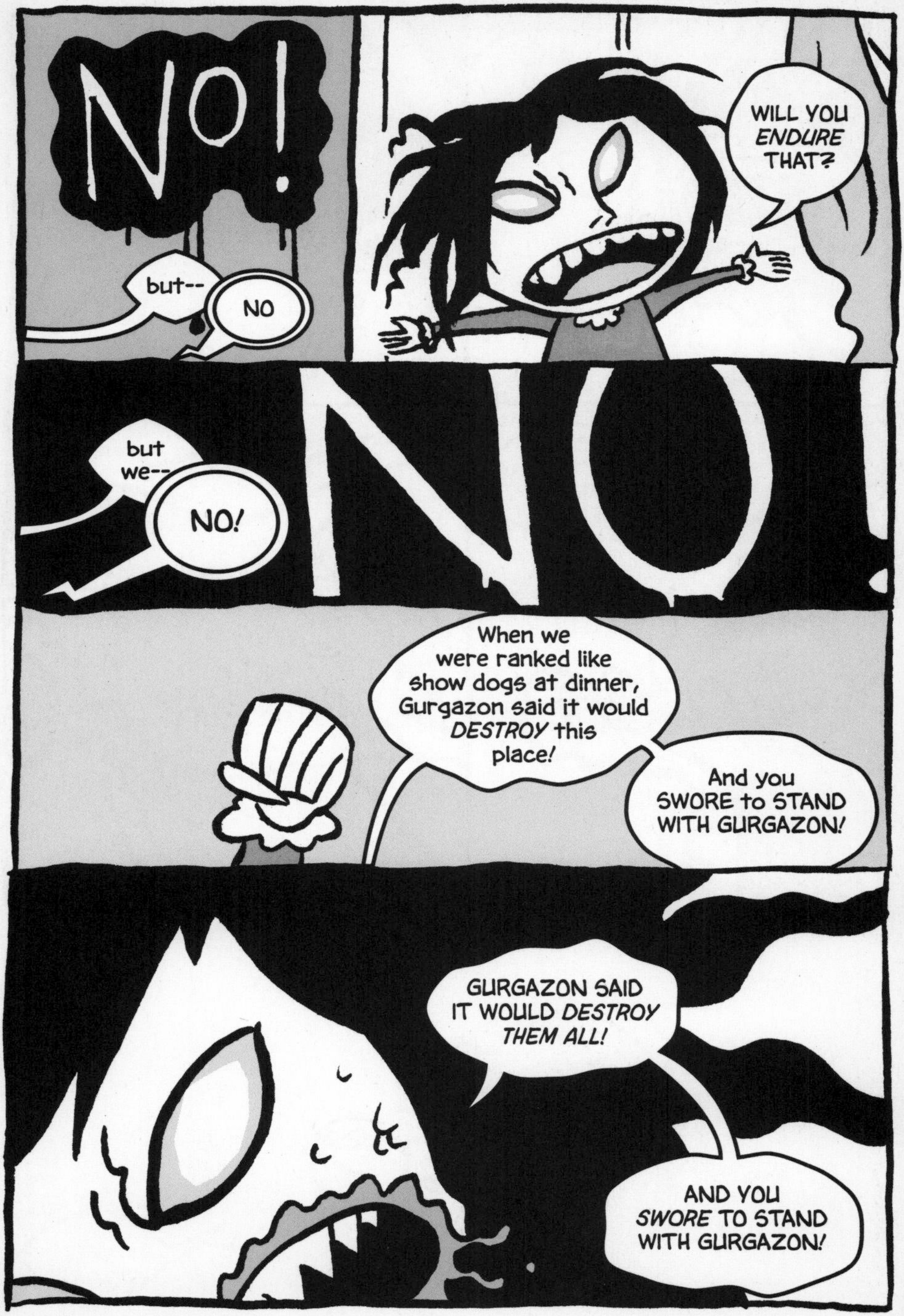
NO!
but--
NO
WILL YOU *ENDURE* THAT?
but we--
NO!
NO!
When we were ranked like show dogs at dinner, Gurgazon said it would *DESTROY* this place!
And you SWORE to STAND WITH GURGAZON!
GURGAZON SAID IT WOULD *DESTROY THEM ALL!*
AND YOU *SWORE* TO STAND WITH GURGAZON!

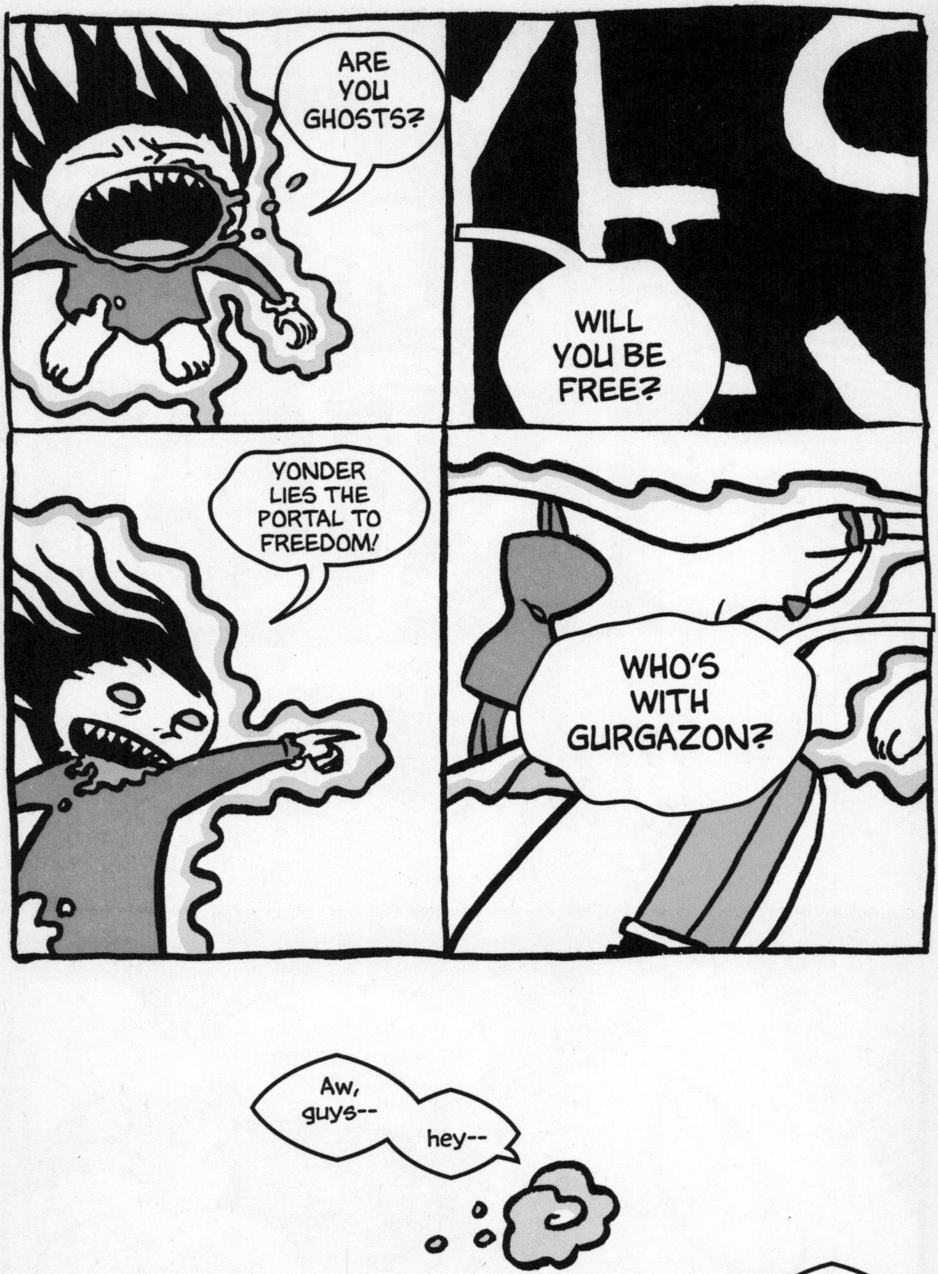
ARE YOU GHOSTS?
WILL YOU BE FREE?
YONDER LIES THE PORTAL TO FREEDOM!
WHO'S WITH GURGAZON?
Aw, guys--
hey--
aw, geez--

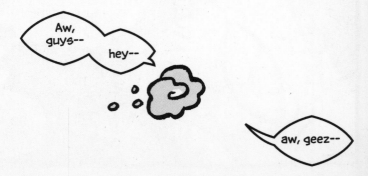

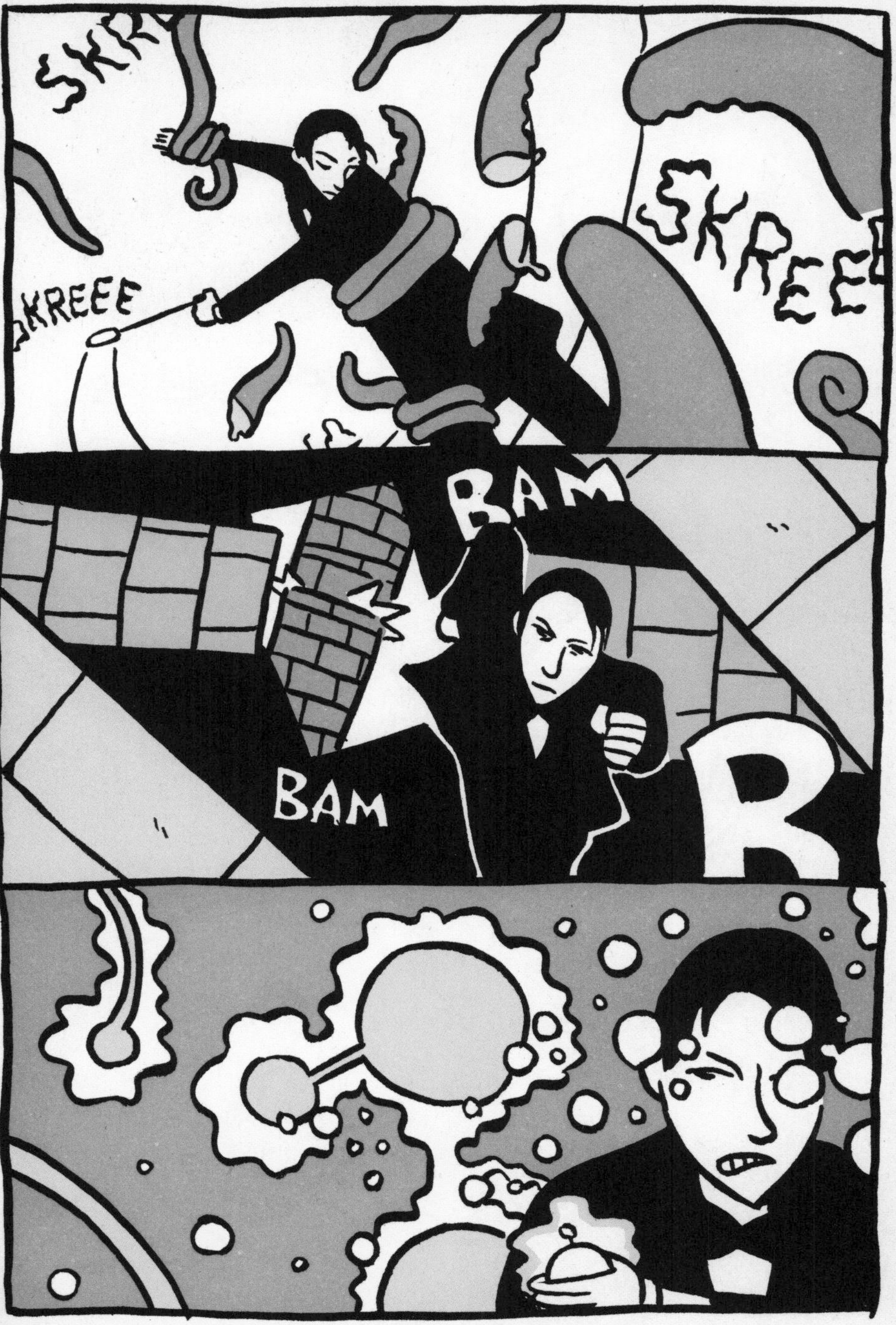
SKR
SKREE
KREEE
BAM
BAM
R

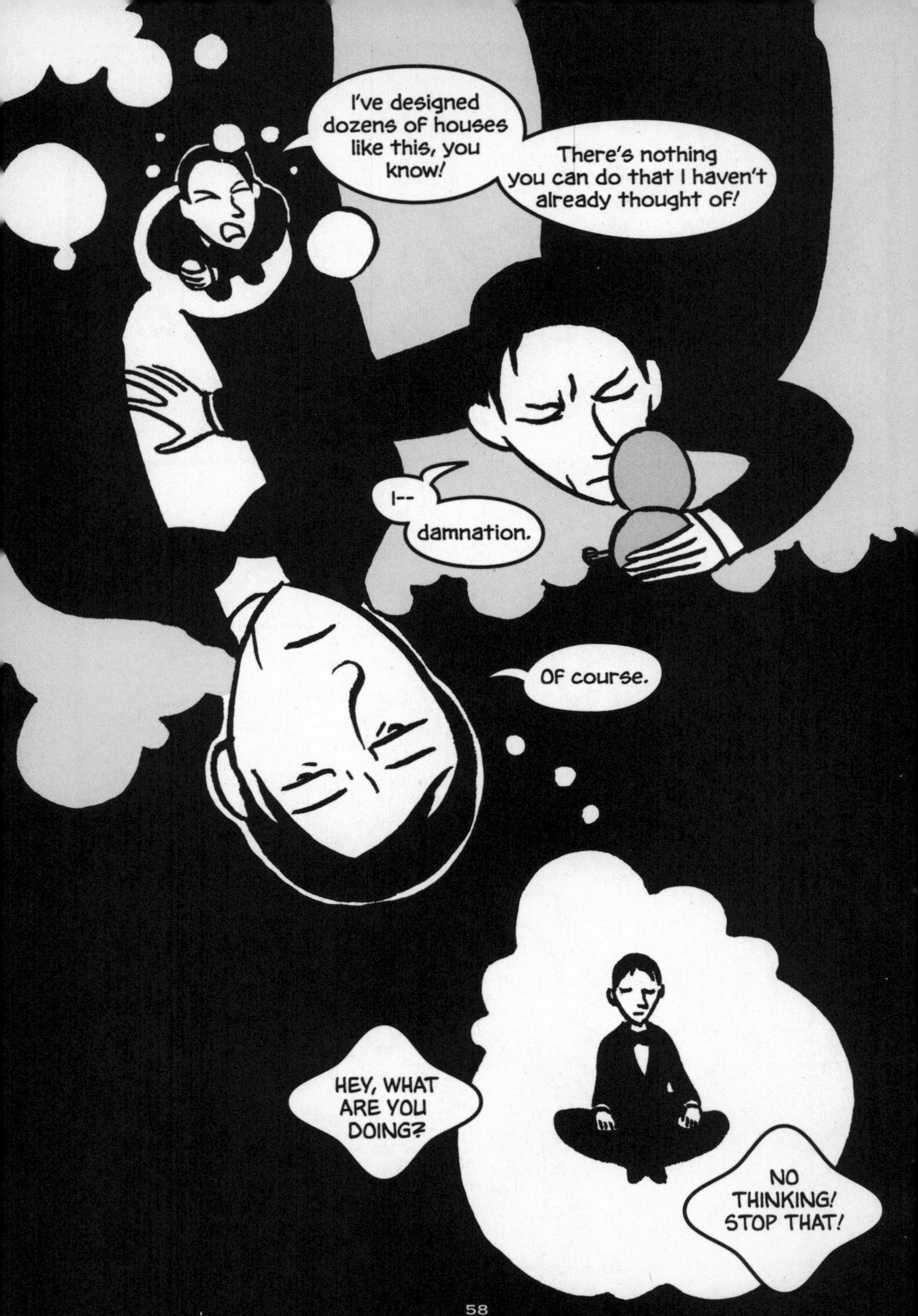
I've designed dozens of houses like this, you know!
There's nothing you can do that I haven't already thought of!
I--
damnation.
Of course.
HEY, WHAT ARE YOU DOING?
NO THINKING! STOP THAT!

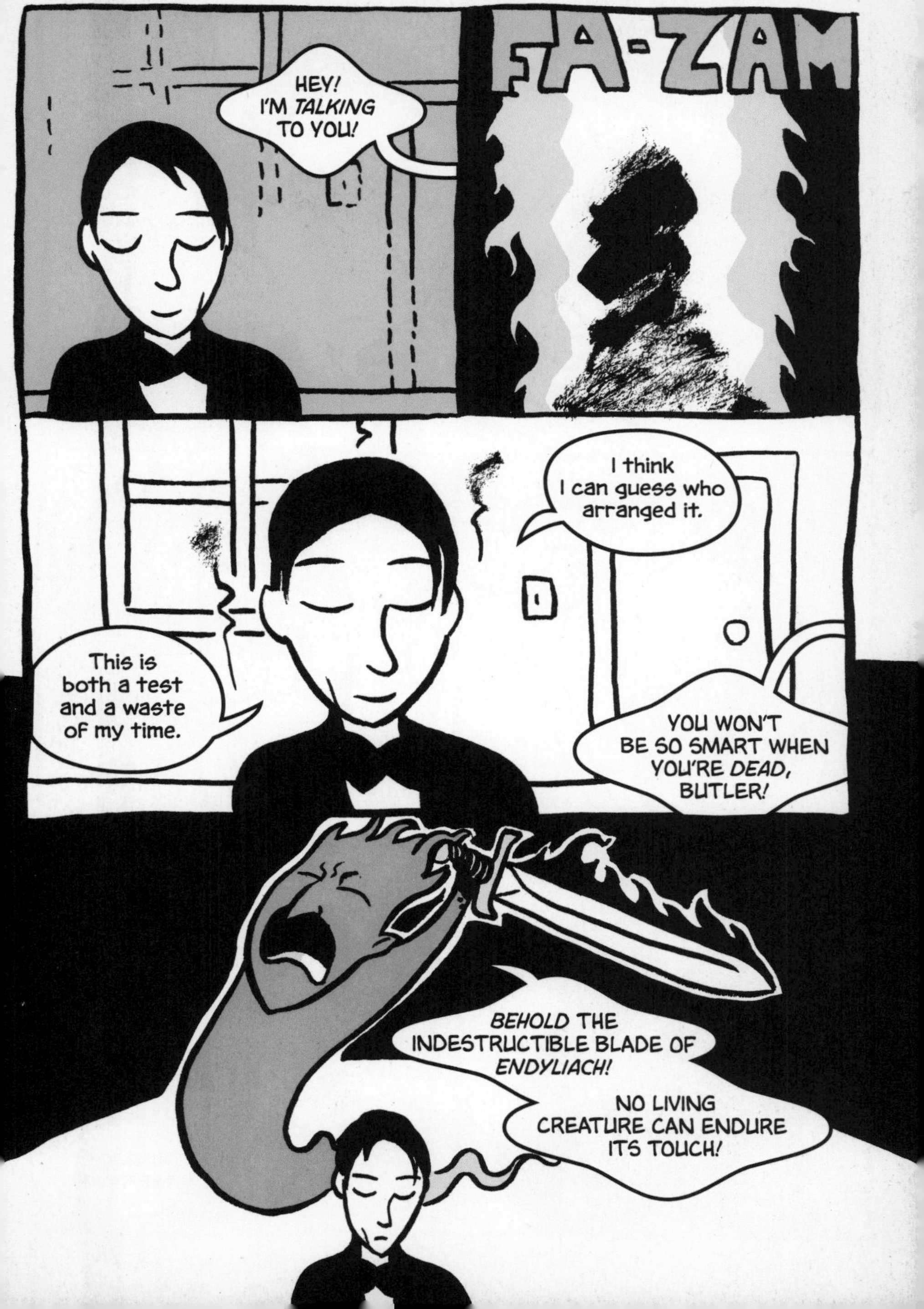
HEY! I'M *TALKING* TO YOU!
FA-ZAM
I think I can guess who arranged it.
This is both a test and a waste of my time.
YOU WON'T BE SO SMART WHEN YOU'RE *DEAD*, BUTLER!
BEHOLD THE INDESTRUCTIBLE BLADE OF *ENDYLIACH!*
NO LIVING CREATURE CAN ENDURE ITS TOUCH!

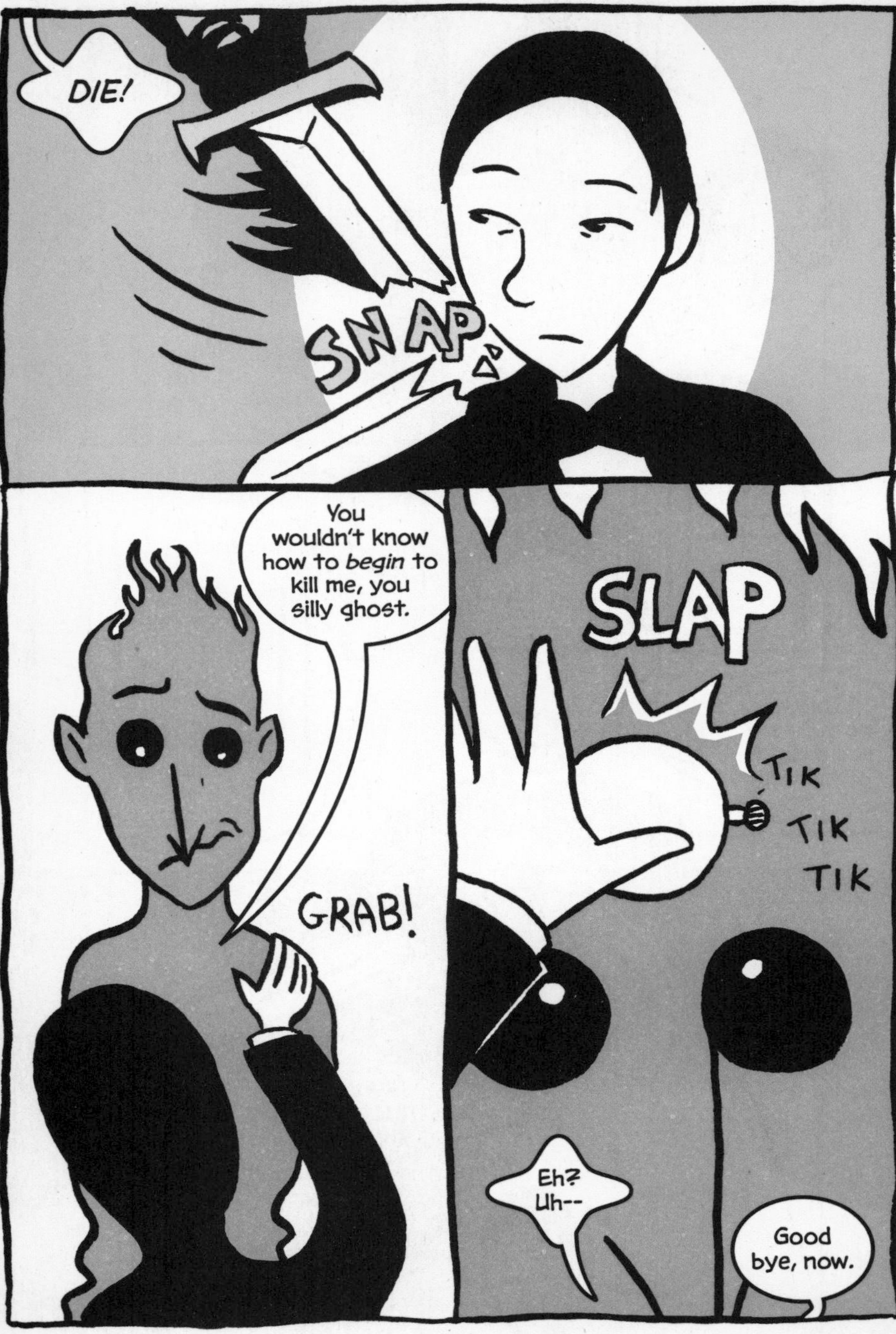
DIE!
SNAP
You wouldn't know how to *begin* to kill me, you silly ghost.
GRAB!
SLAP
TIK
TIK
TIK
Eh? Uh--
Good bye, now.

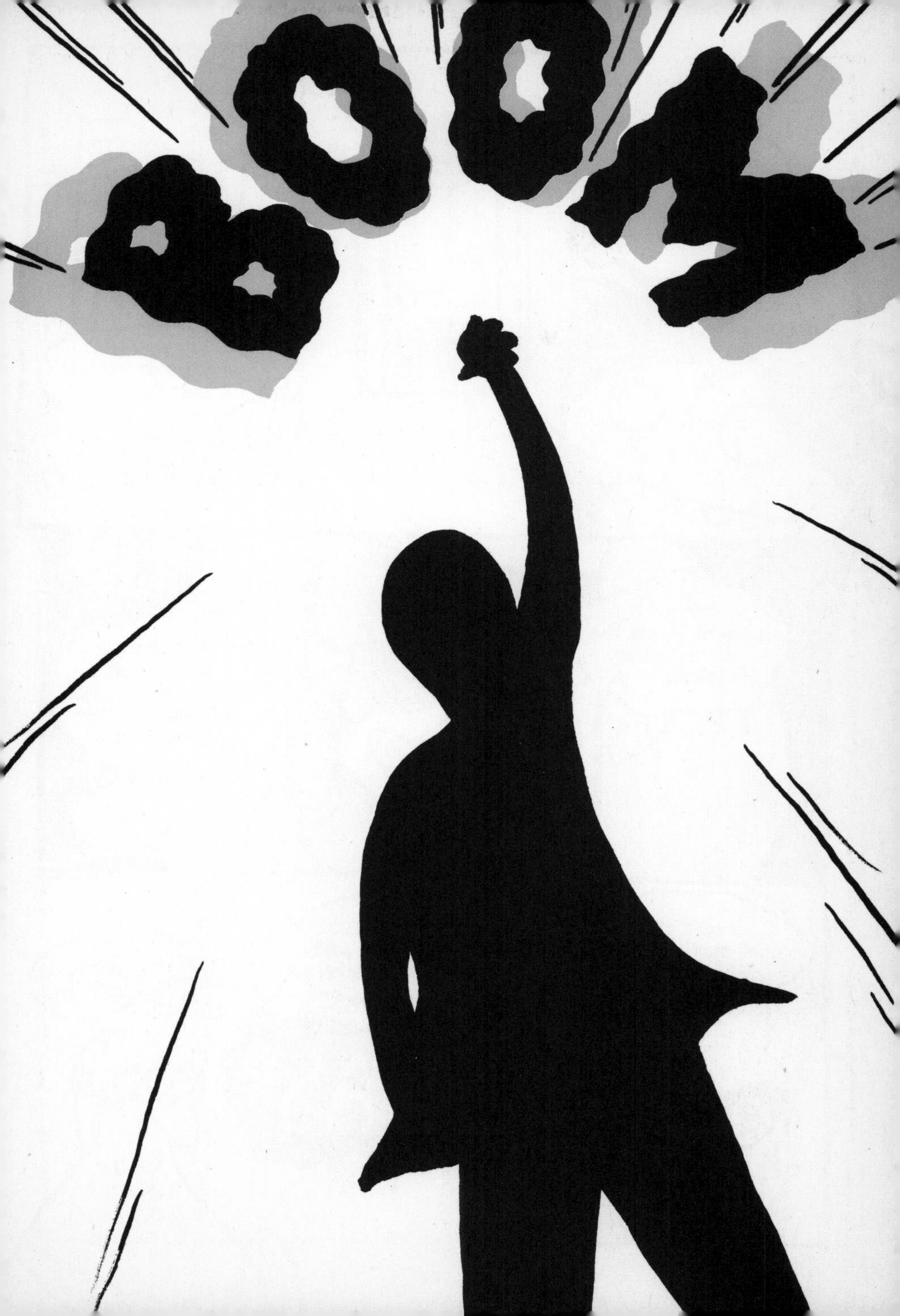
BOOM

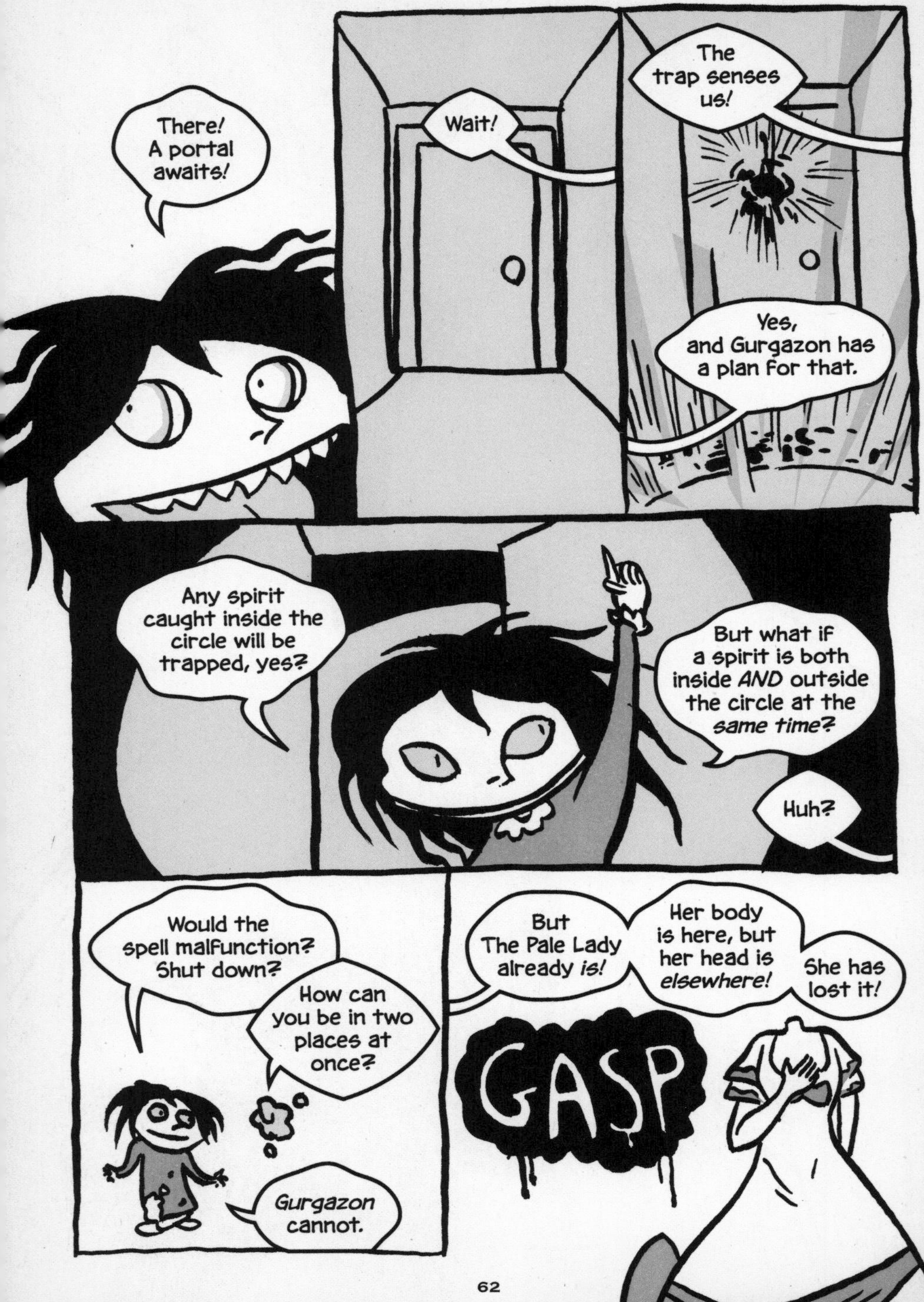

There! A portal awaits!
Wait!
The trap senses us!
Yes, and Gurgazon has a plan for that.
Any spirit caught inside the circle will be trapped, yes?
But what if a spirit is both inside *AND* outside the circle at the *same time*?
Huh?
Would the spell malfunction? Shut down?
How can you be in two places at once?
Gurgazon cannot.
But The Pale Lady already *is!*
Her body is here, but her head is *elsewhere!*
She has lost it!
GASP

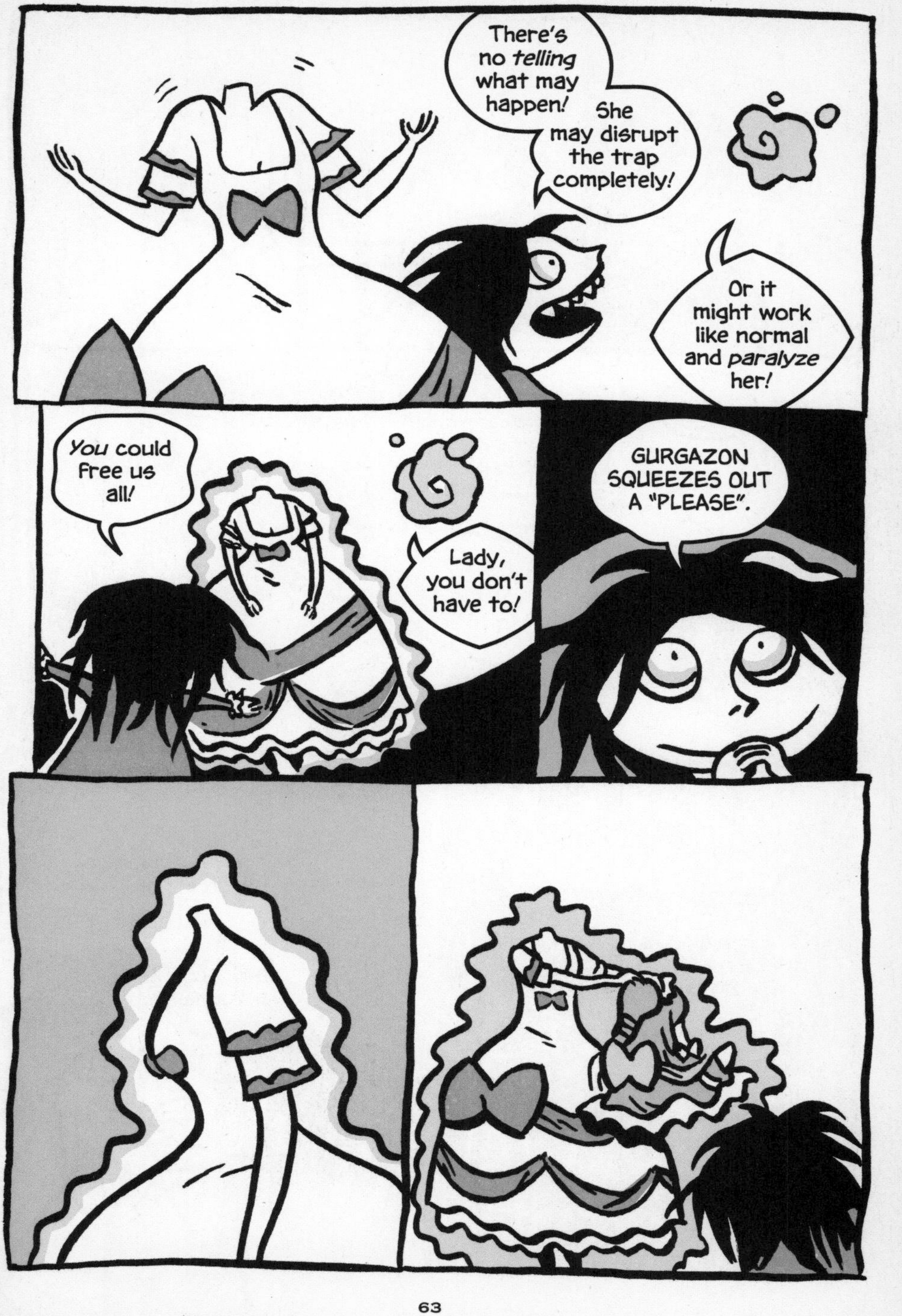
There's no *telling* what may happen!
She may disrupt the trap completely!
Or it might work like normal and *paralyze* her!
You could free us all!
Lady, you don't have to!
GURGAZON SQUEEZES OUT A "PLEASE".

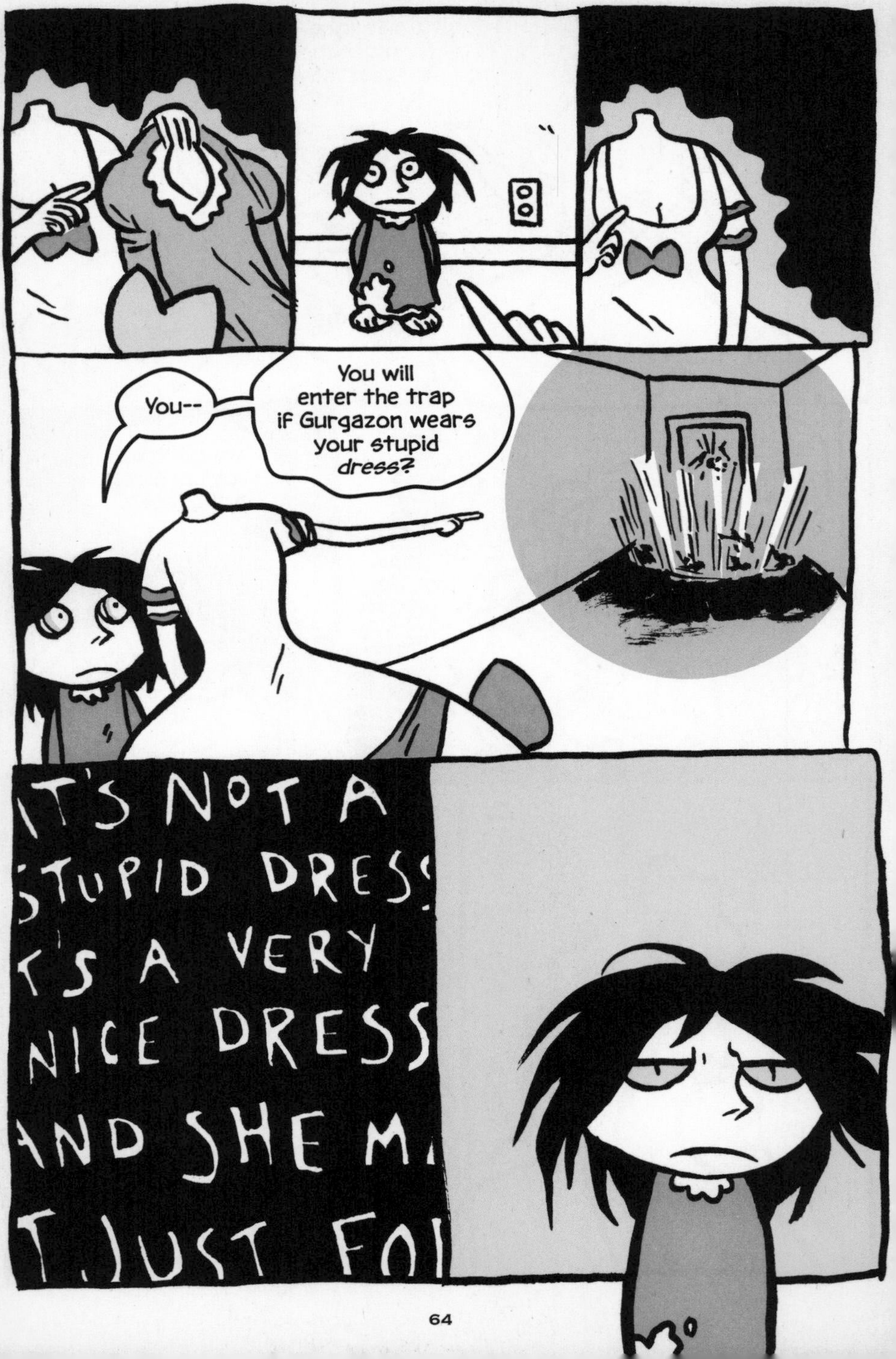
You--
You will enter the trap if Gurgazon wears your stupid dress?
IT'S NOT A STUPID DRESS IT'S A VERY NICE DRESS AND SHE MA T JUST FO

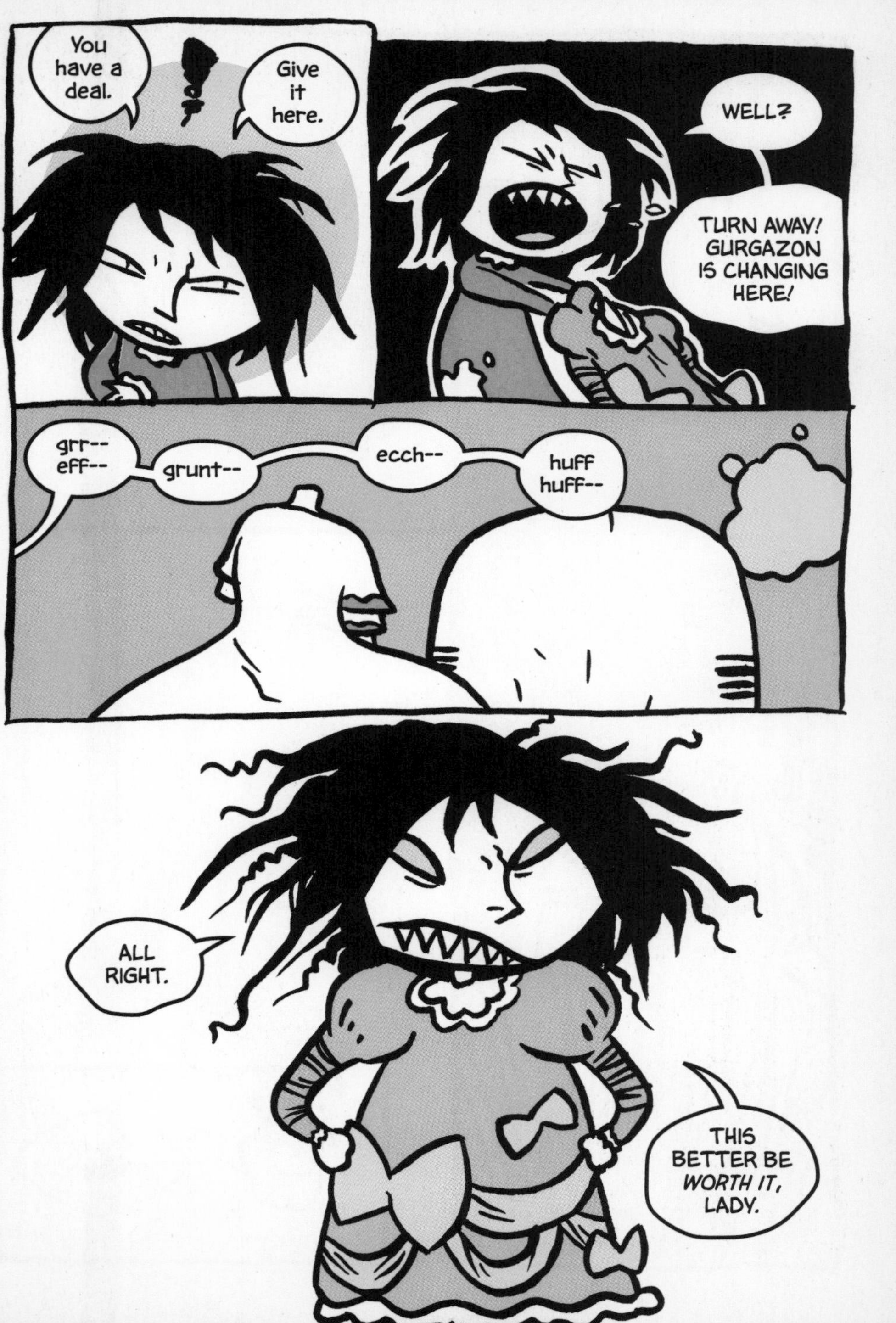
You have a deal.
Give it here.
WELL?
TURN AWAY! GURGAZON IS CHANGING HERE!
grr-- eff--
grunt--
ecch--
huff huff--
ALL RIGHT.
THIS BETTER BE *WORTH IT*, LADY.

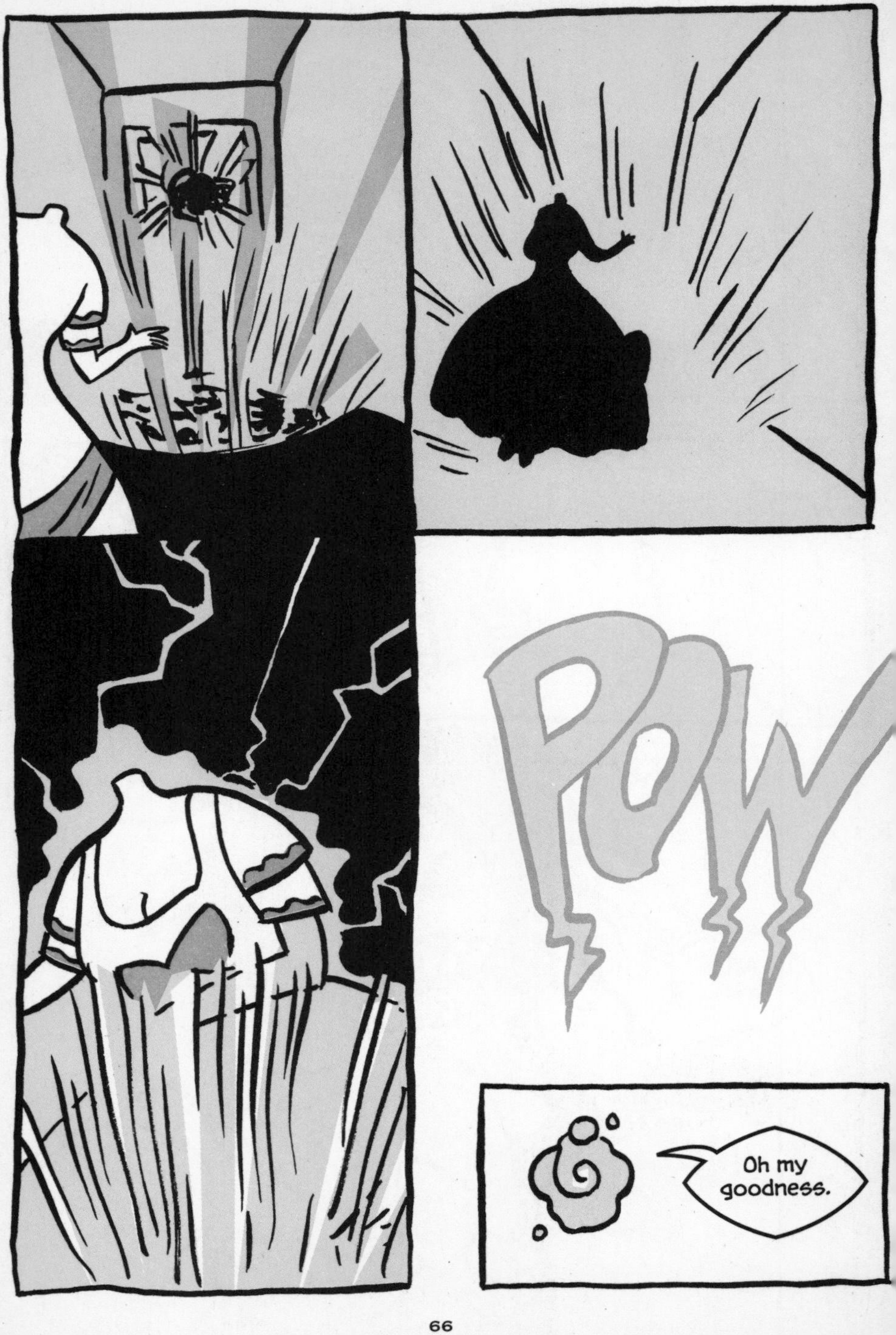
POW
Oh my goodness.

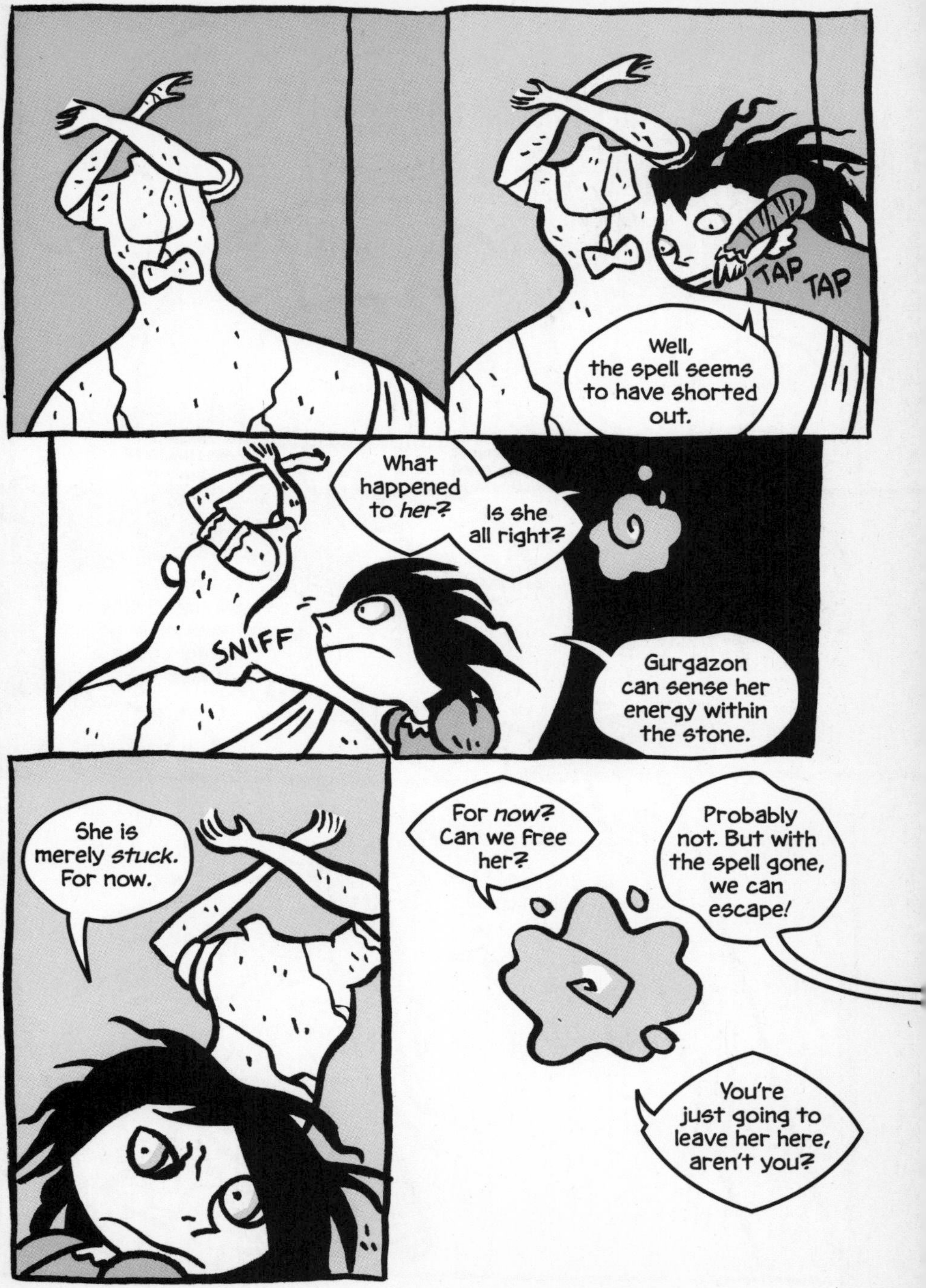
TAP TAP
Well, the spell seems to have shorted out.
What happened to *her*?
Is she all right?
SNIFF
Gurgazon can sense her energy within the stone.
She is merely *stuck*. For now.
For *now*? Can we free her?
Probably not. But with the spell gone, we can *escape!*
You're just going to leave her here, aren't you?

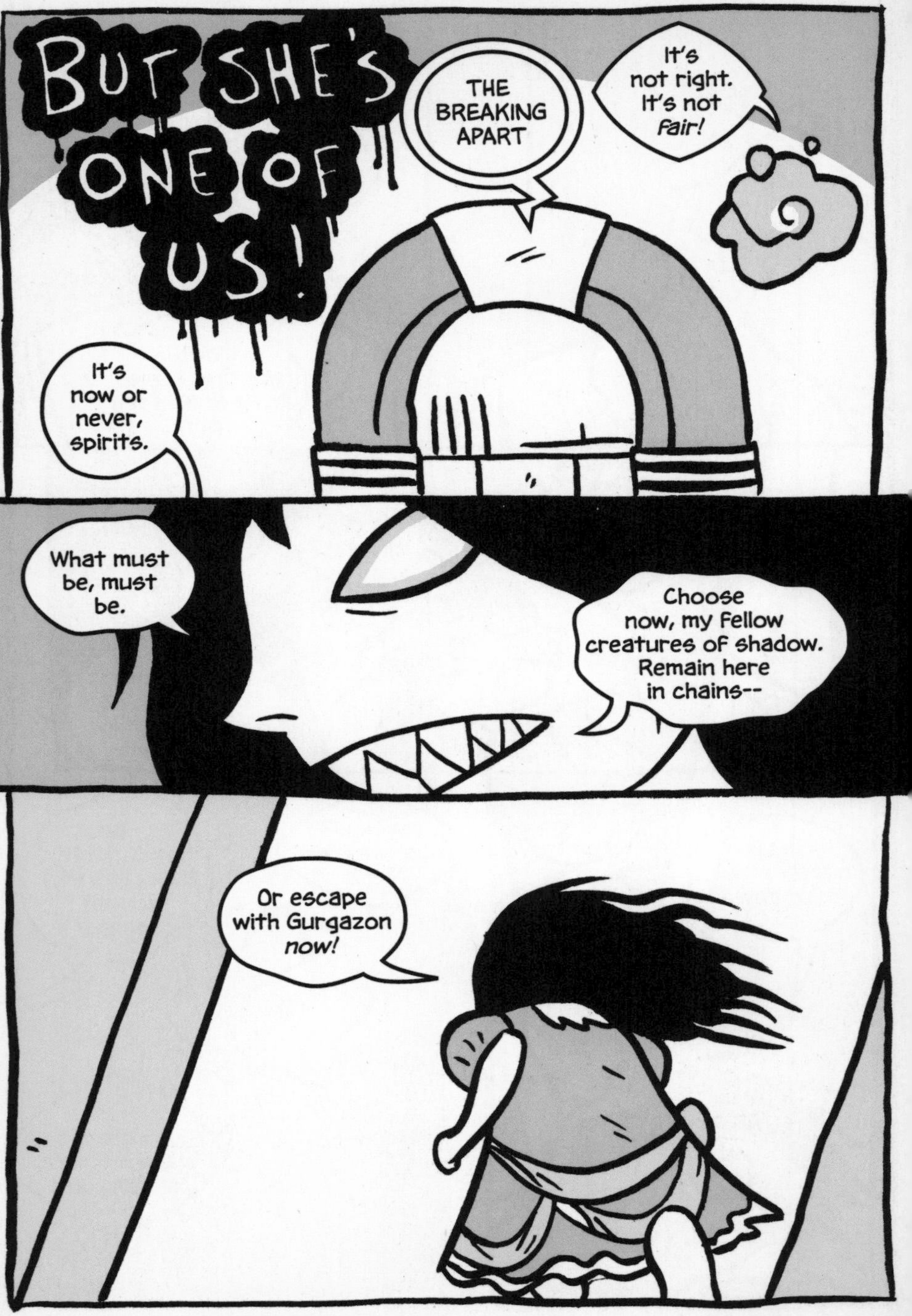
BUT SHE'S ONE OF US!
THE BREAKING APART
It's not right. It's not *fair!*
It's now or never, spirits.
What must be, must be.
Choose now, my fellow creatures of shadow. Remain here in chains--
Or escape with Gurgazon *now!*

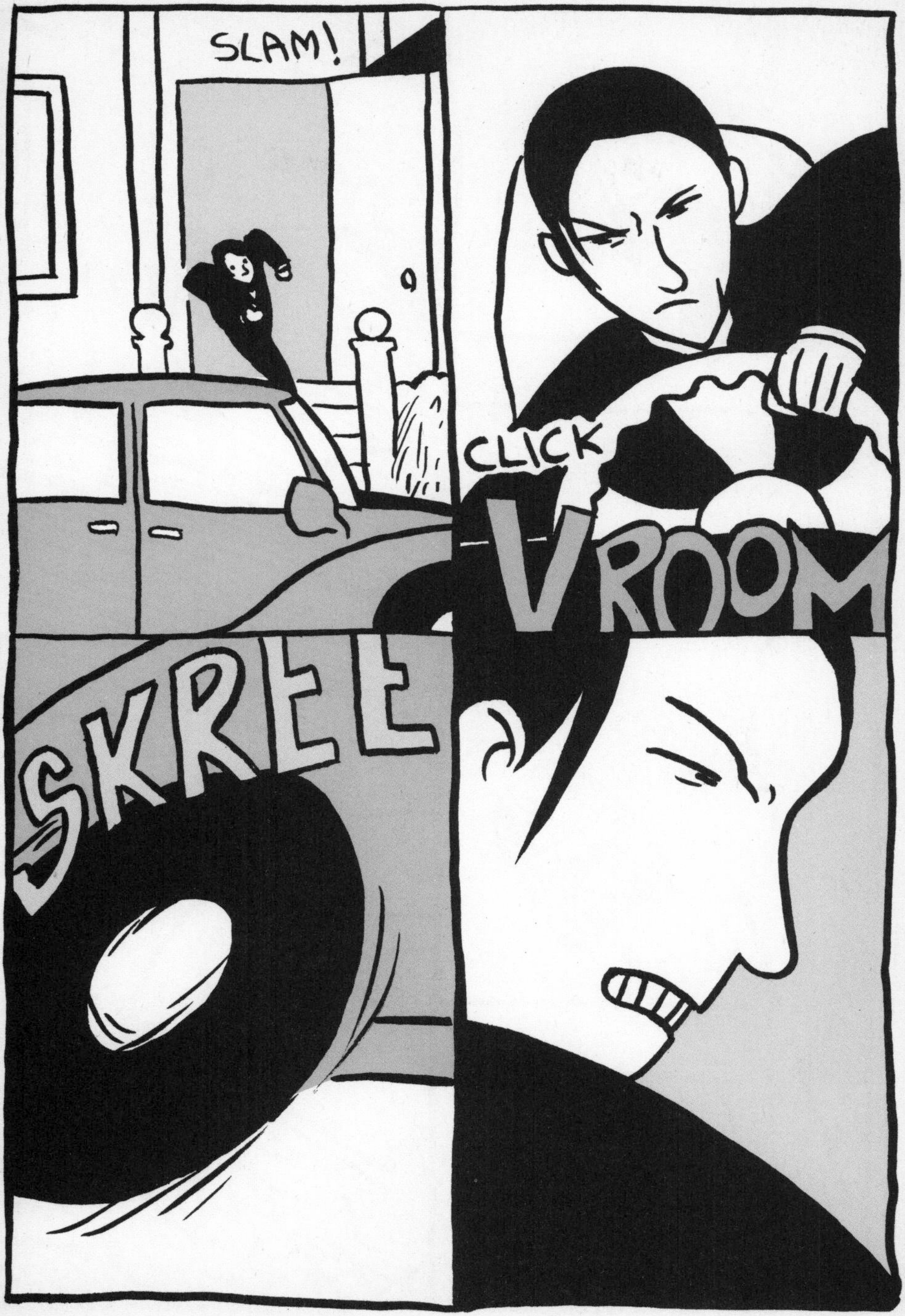
SLAM!
CLICK
VROOM
SKREE

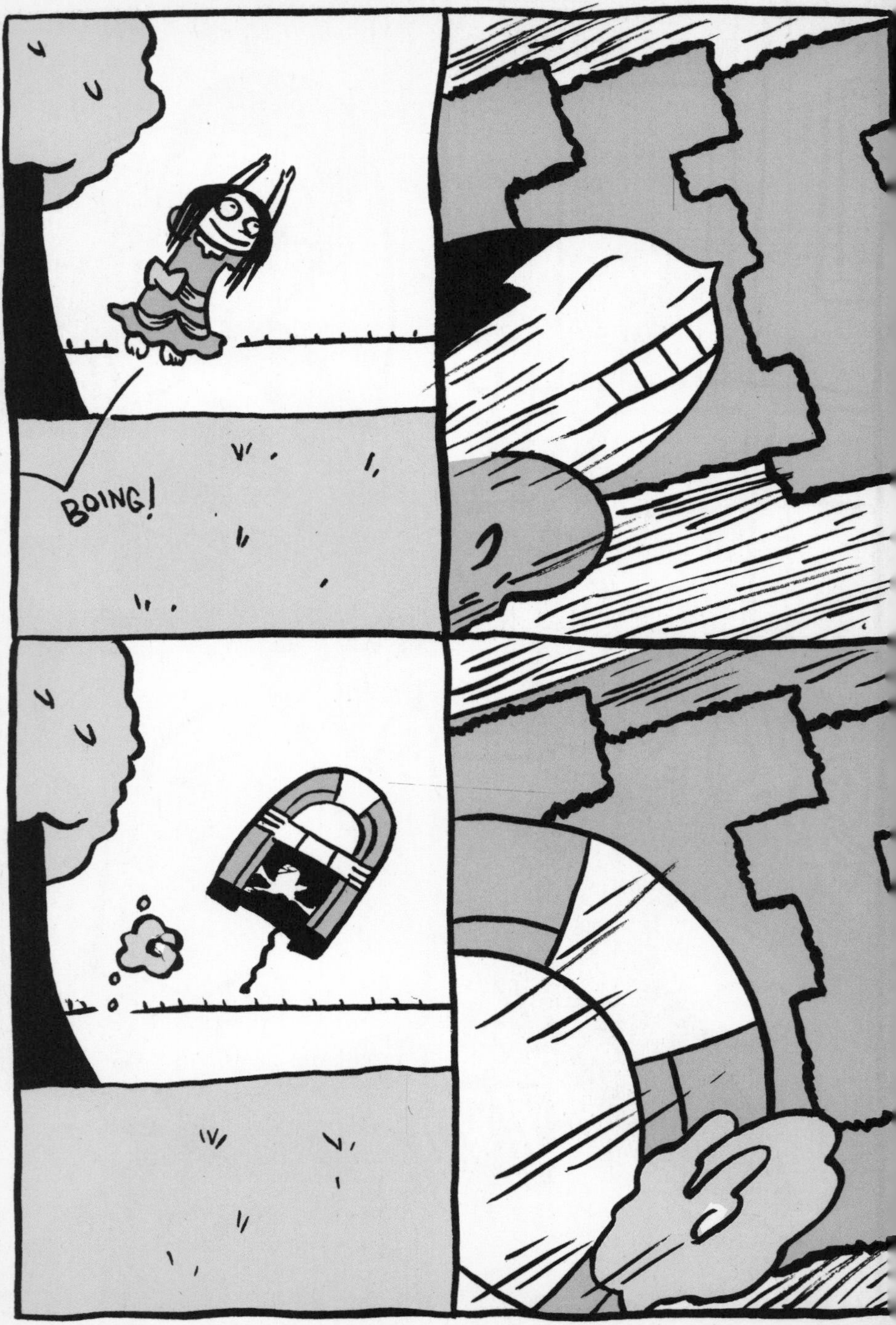
BOING!

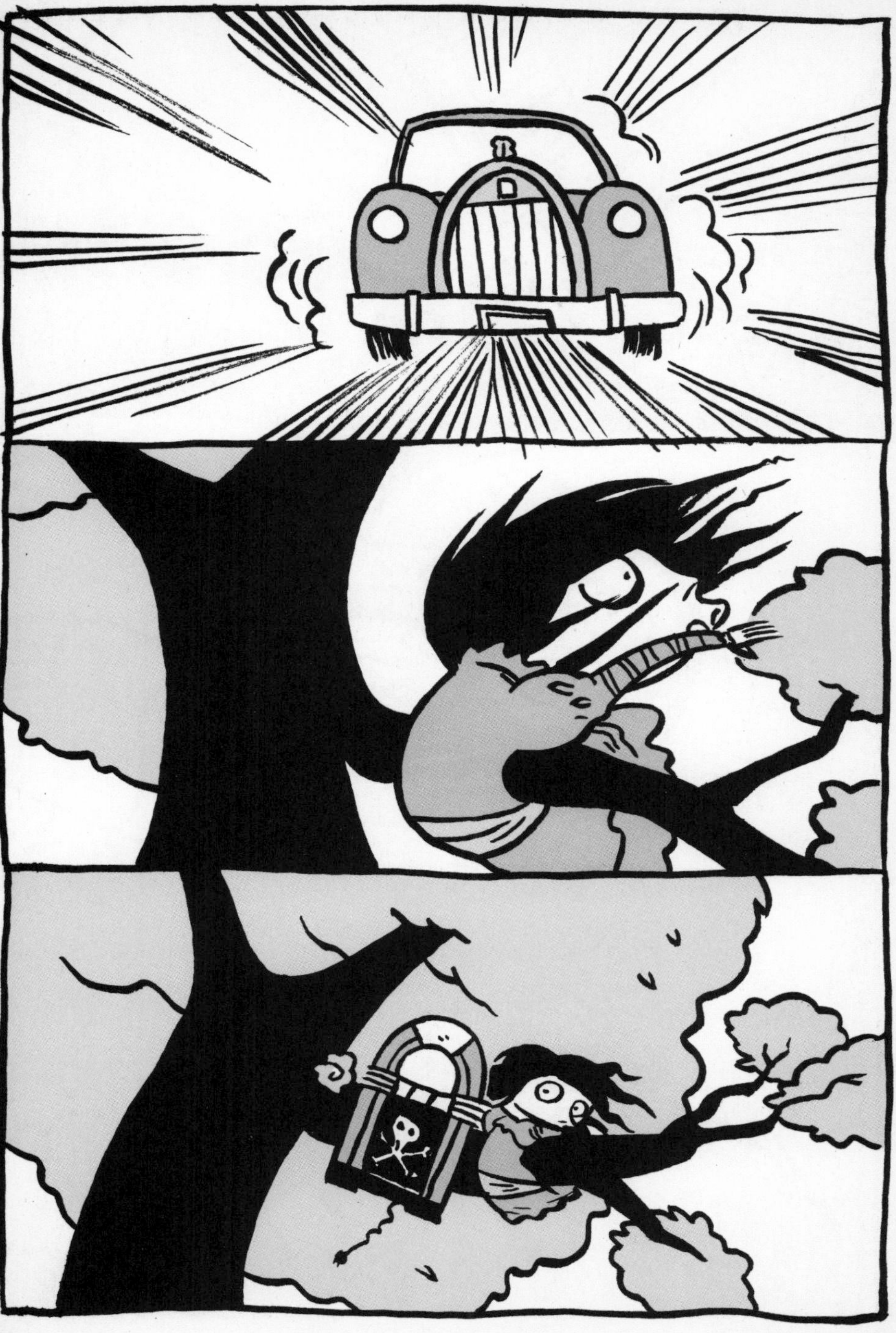

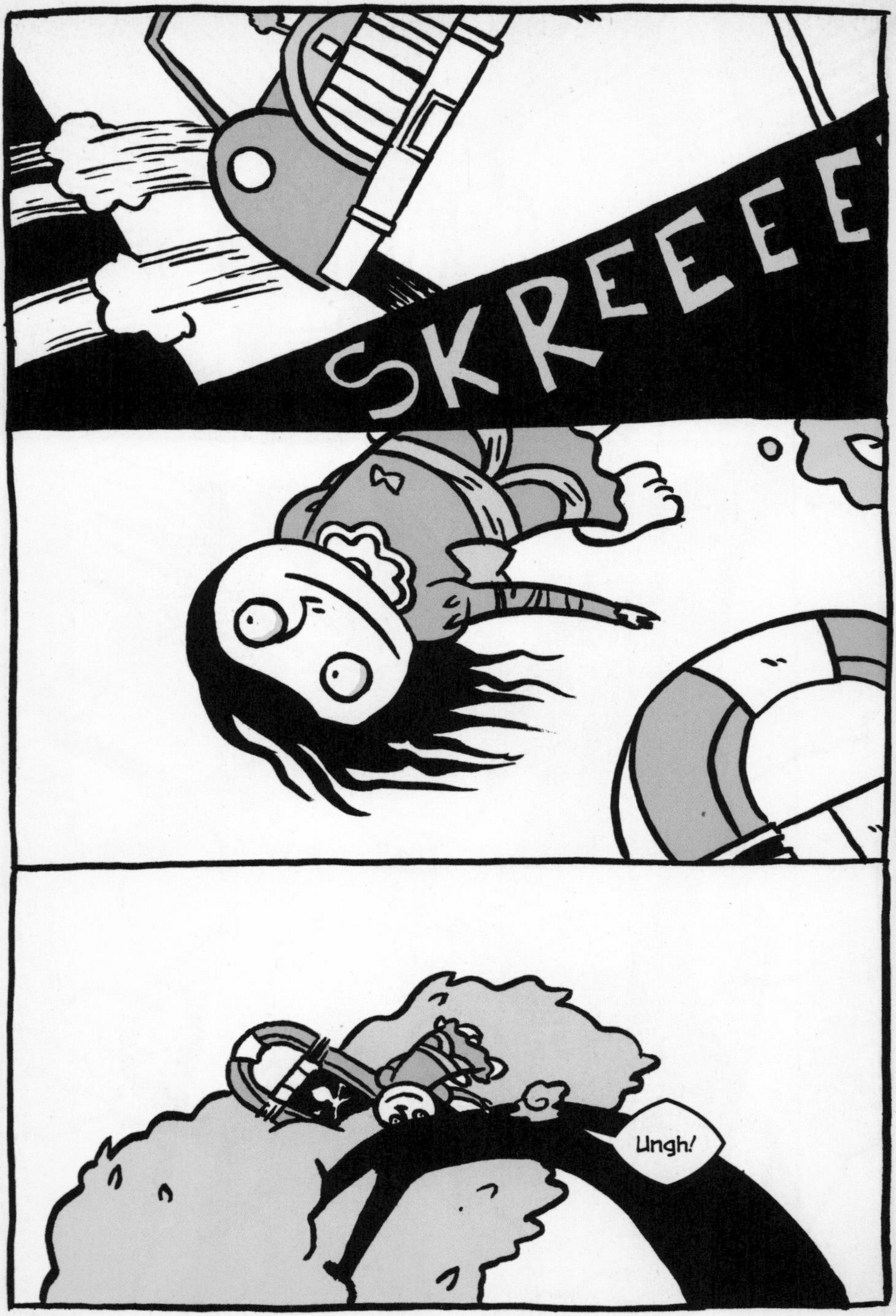
SKREEEE
Ungh!

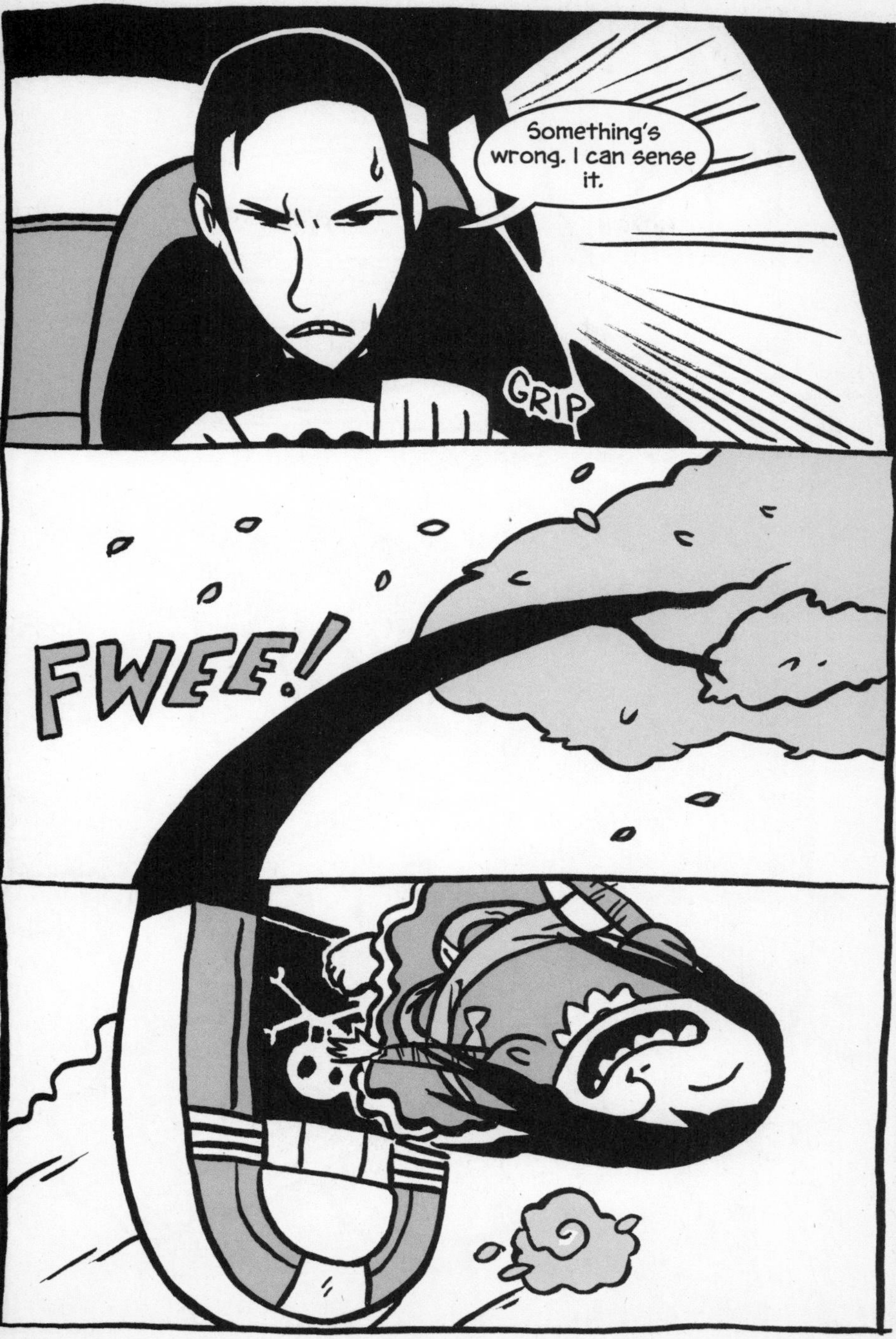
Something's wrong. I can sense it.
GRIP
FWEE!

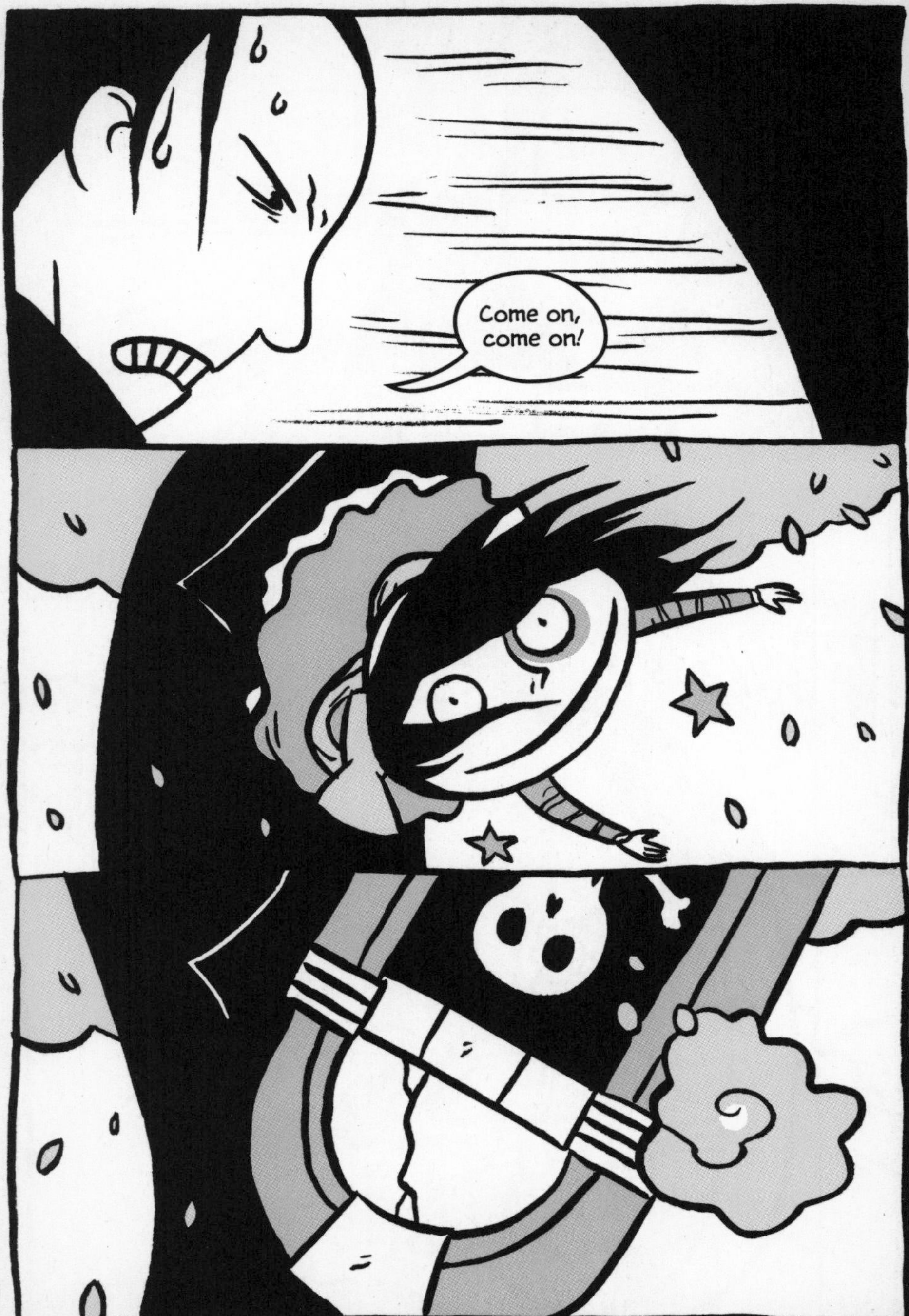
Come on, come on!

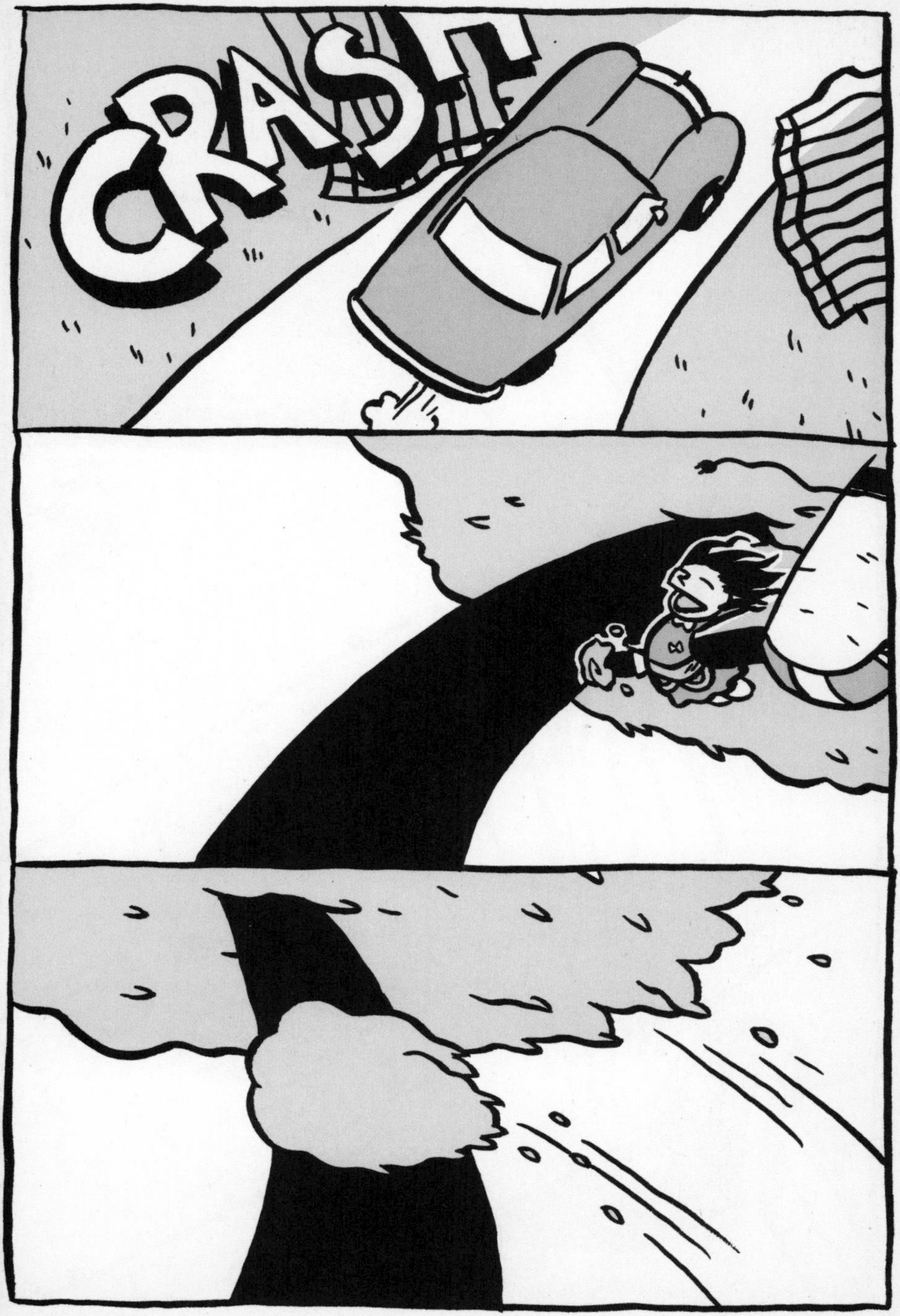
CRASH

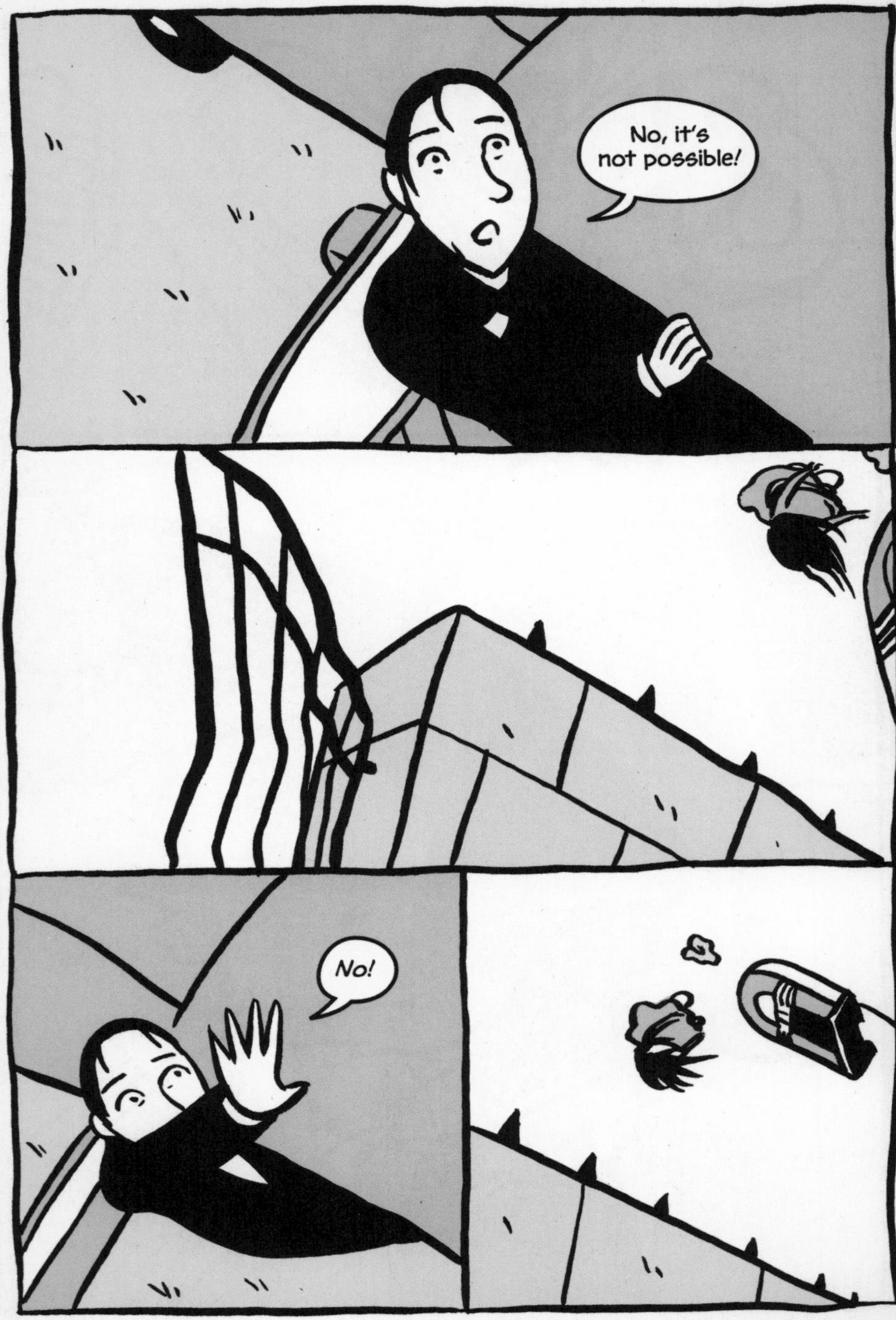
No, it's not possible!
No!

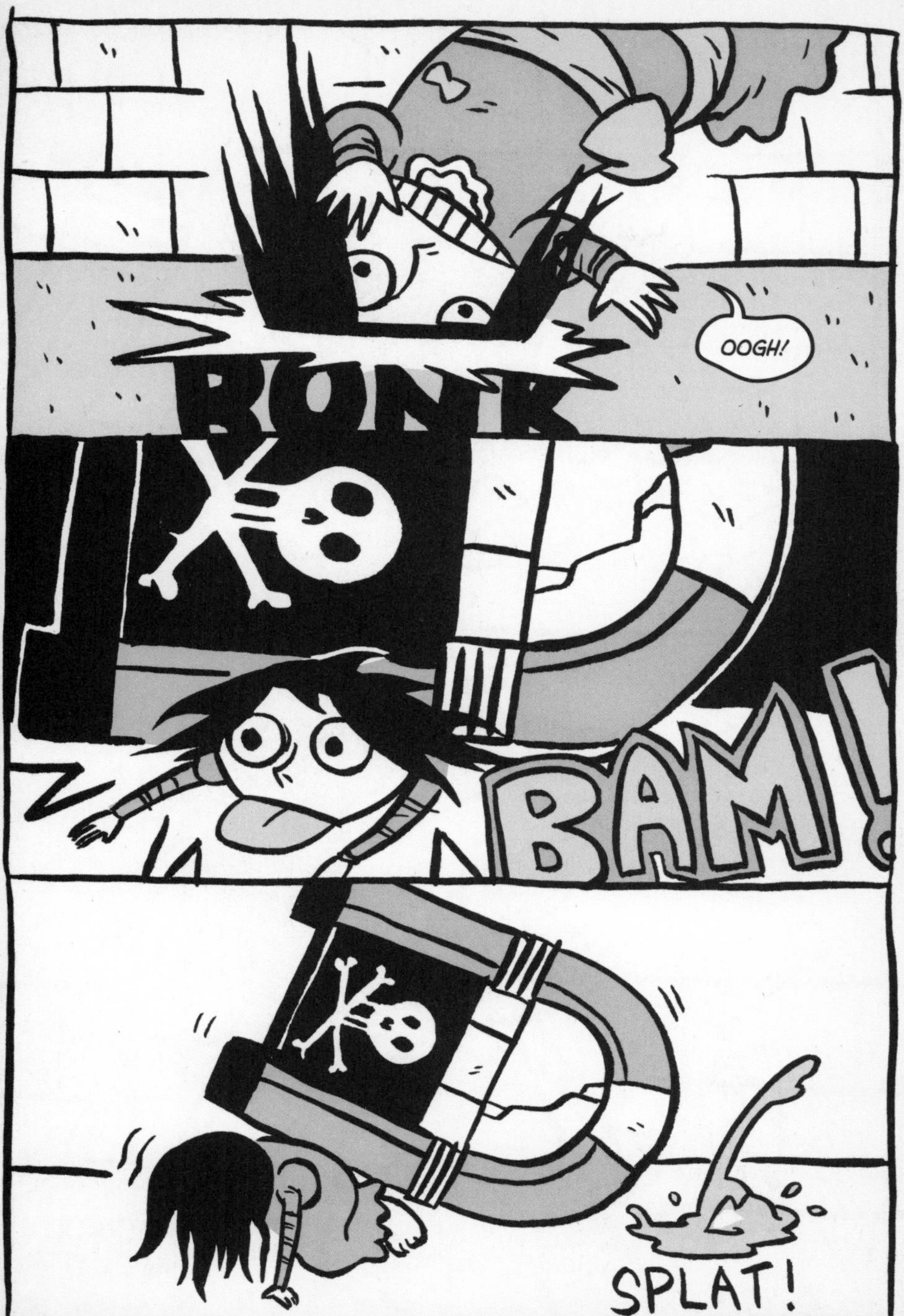
OOGH!
BONK
BAM!
SPLAT!

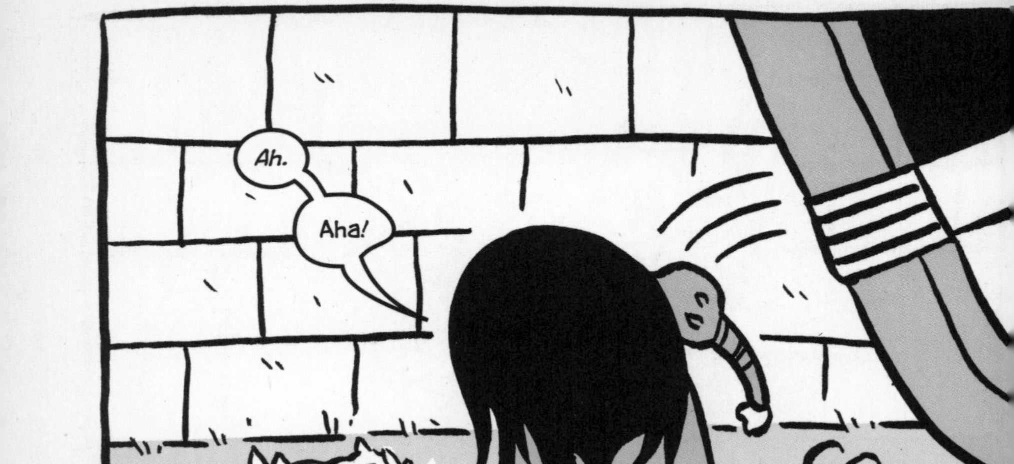
Ah.
Aha!
DID WE DO IT?
CRASH!

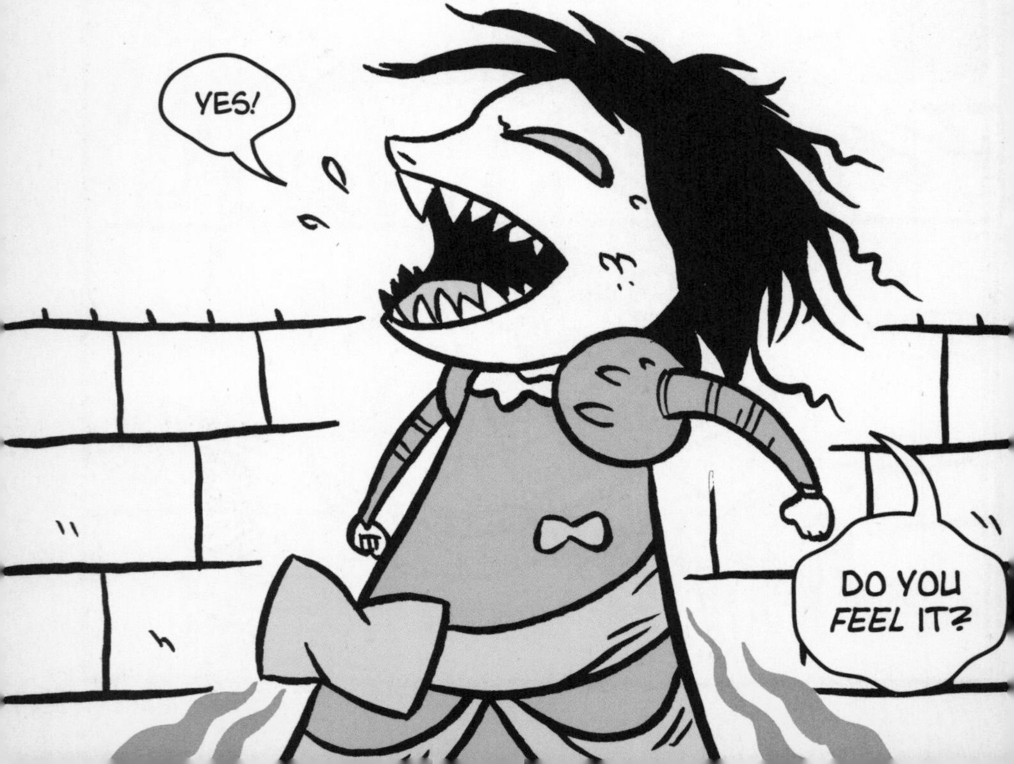
YES!
DO YOU FEEL IT?

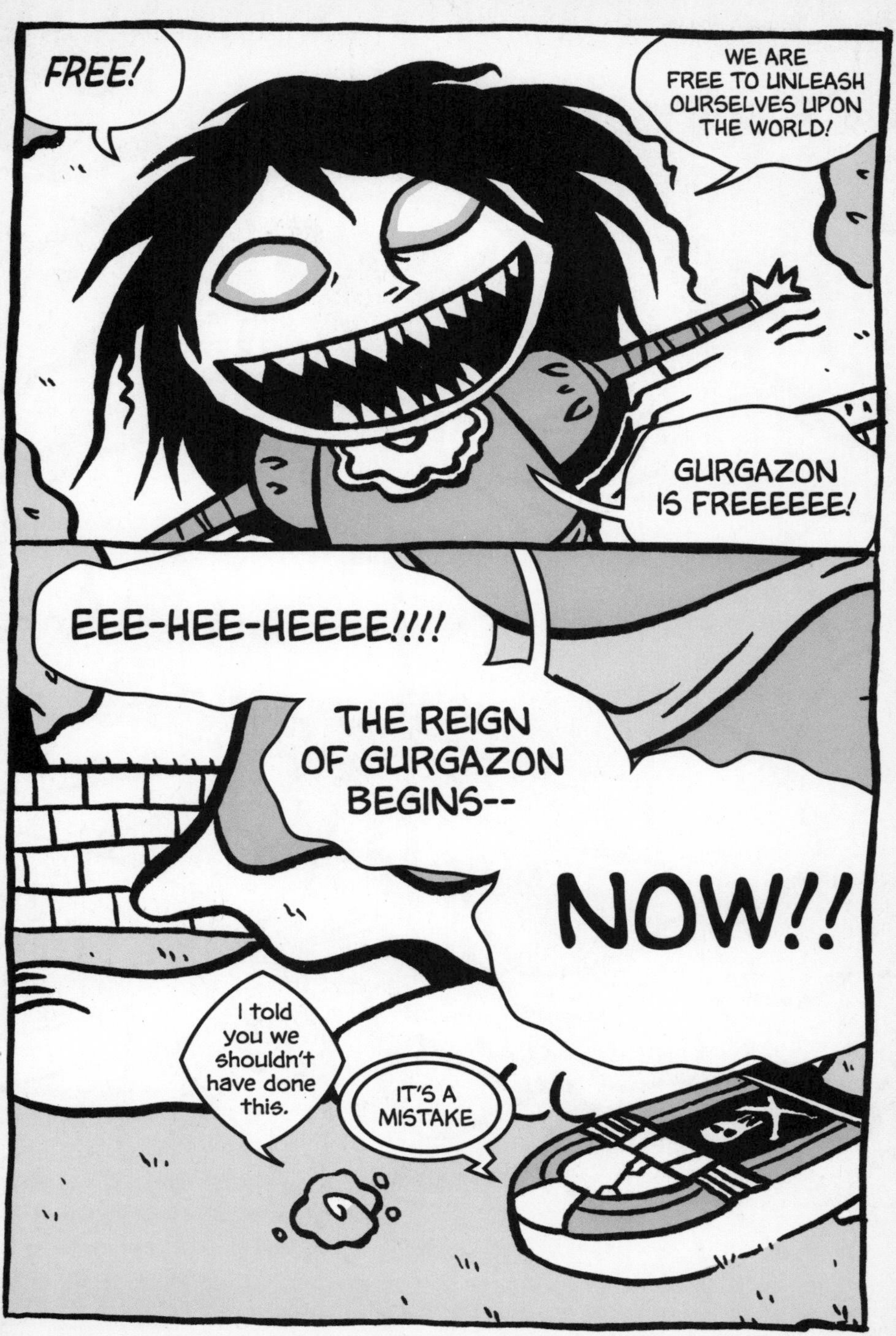
FREE!
WE ARE FREE TO UNLEASH OURSELVES UPON THE WORLD!
GURGAZON IS FREEEEEEE!
EEE-HEE-HEEEEE!!!!
THE REIGN OF GURGAZON BEGINS--
NOW!!
I told you we shouldn't have done this.
IT'S A MISTAKE

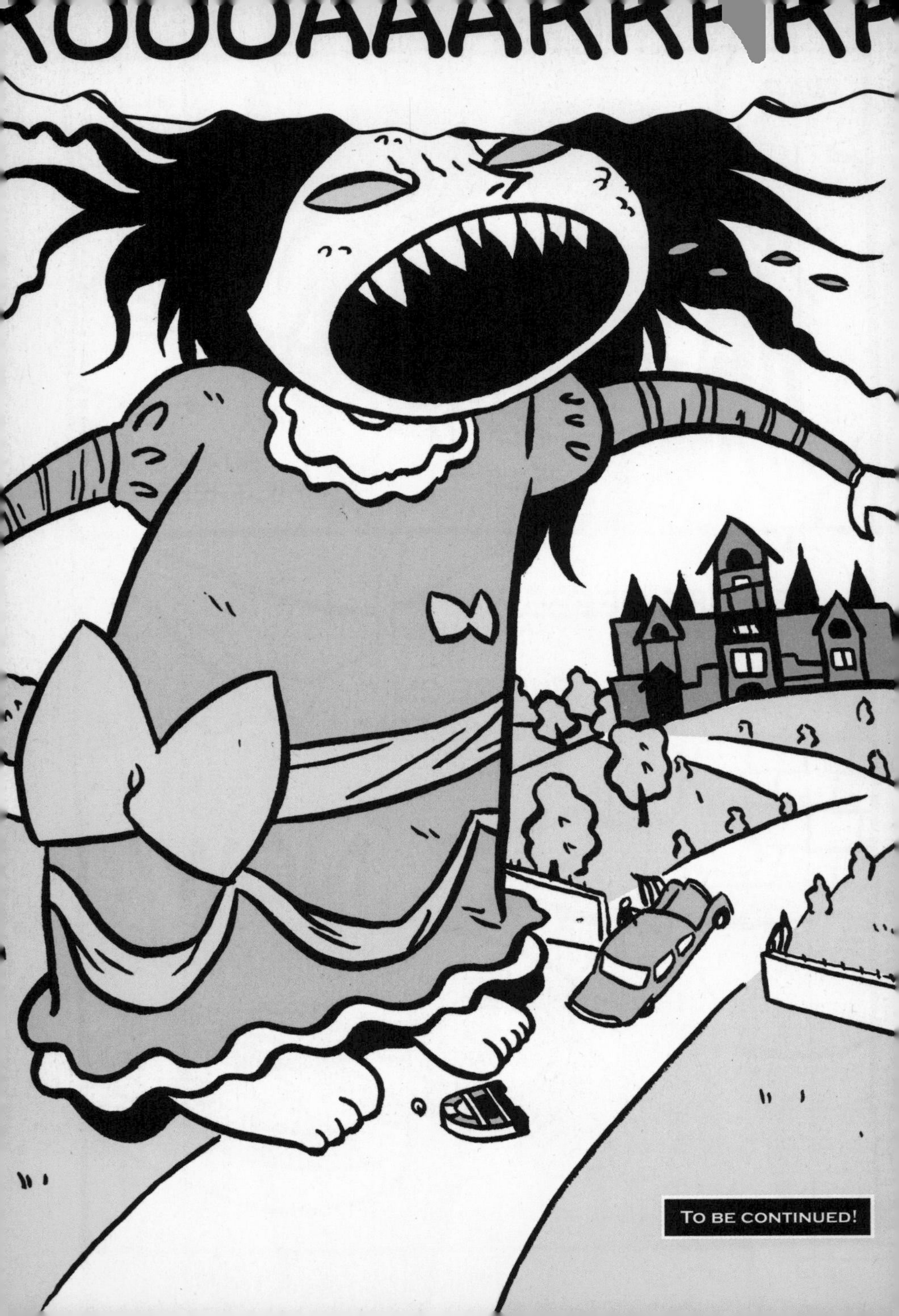
ROOOAAARRRRR
TO BE CONTINUED!

POSSESSIONS

BOOK THREE

AUTHOR BIO

RAY FAWKES is a critically acclaimed writer and artist based in Toronto, Canada. His work has appeared online and in print around the world, and he is a two-time nominee for a Shuster award as "Outstanding Canadian Comic Book Writer." He ranges in style from dark, visceral horror (*Mnemovore*, *Black Strings*) to slapstick and black humor (*The Apocalipstix*), and has been published by DC/Vertigo, Oni Press, Tor.com, Top Shelf 2.0, White Wolf Publishing, and more.

www.rayfawkes.com

OTHER BOOKS FROM ONI PRESS

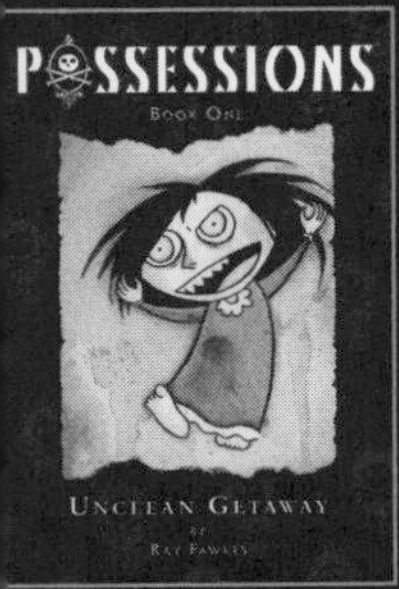
POSSESSIONS
Book One
Unclean Getaway

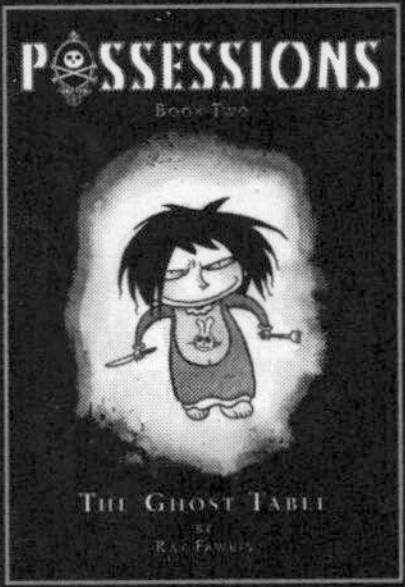
POSSESSIONS
The Ghost Table

POSSESSIONS, BOOK ONE:
UNCLEAN GETAWAY
By Ray Fawkes
88 pages · 6x9
black and white and sickly green interior
$5.99 US
ISBN 978-1-934964-36-1

POSSESSIONS, BOOK TWO:
THE GHOST TABLE
By Ray Fawkes
88 pages · 6x9
black and white and bone-chilling blue interior
$5.99 US
ISBN 978-1-934964-61-3

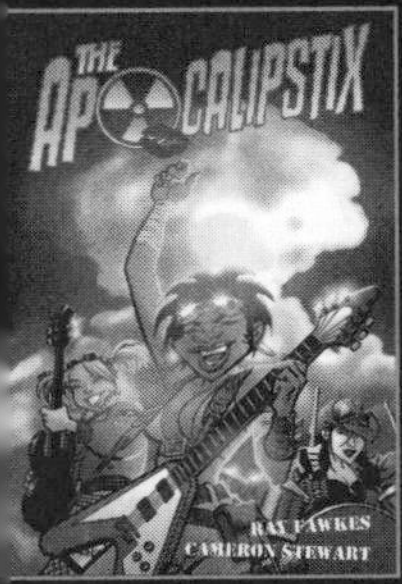
THE APOCALIPSTIX
RAY FAWKES
CAMERON STEWART

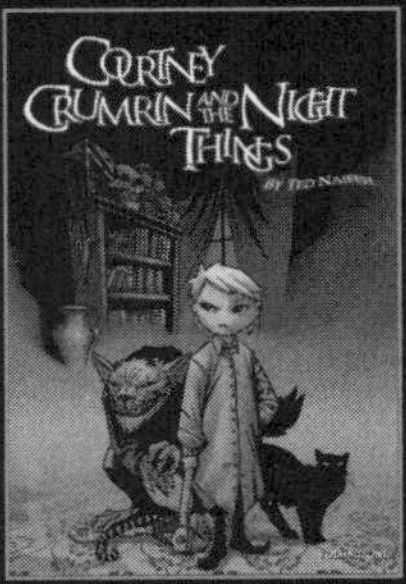
COURTNEY CRUMRIN AND THE NIGHT THINGS

Apocalipstix
Volume 1
By Ray Fawkes & Cameron Stewart
144 pages · digest
black and white
$11.95 US
ISBN 978-1-932664-45-4

Courtney Crumrin
Volume 1: The Night Things
By Ted Naifeh
128 pages · digest
black and white
$11.95 US
ISBN 978-1-929998-60-9

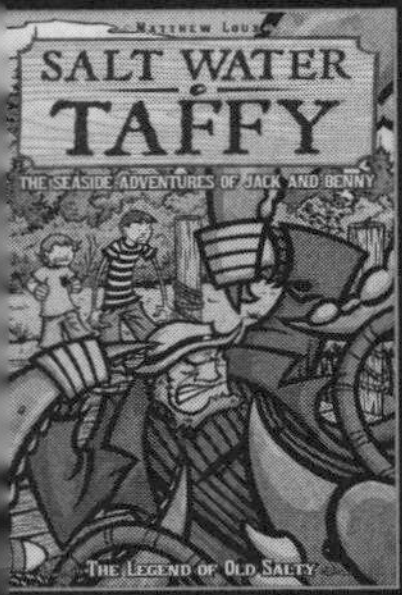
MATTHEW LOUX
SALT WATER TAFFY
THE SEASIDE ADVENTURES OF JACK AND BENNY
THE LEGEND OF OLD SALTY

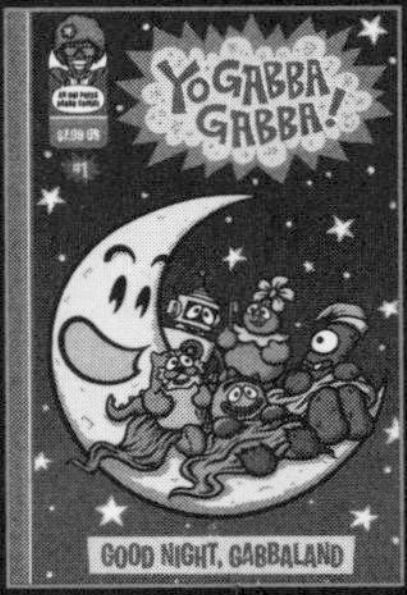
YO GABBA GABBA!
#1
GOOD NIGHT, GABBALAND

Salt Water Taffy, Volume 1 -
The Legend Of Old Salty
By Matthew Loux
96 pages · digest
black and white
$5.95 US
ISBN 978-1-932664-94-2

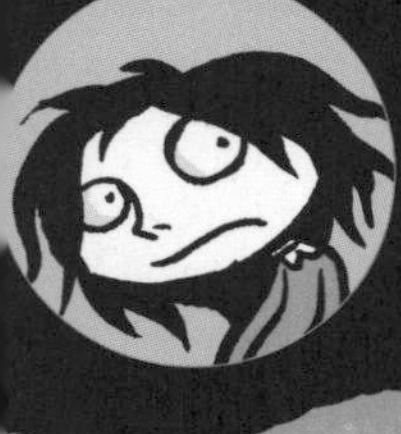

Possessions
Book 4
The Final Tantrum
By Ray Fawkes

Spring 2013!

Yo Gabba Gabba:
Good Night, Gabbaland
By J. Torres & Matthew Loux
16 pages · board comic
full color
$7.99 US
ISBN 978-1-934964-56-9

more information on these and other fine Oni Press comic books and graphic
els, visit www.onipress.com. To find a comic specialty store in your area, call
88-COMICBOOK or visit www.comicshops.us.

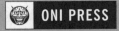

ONI PRESS www.onipress.com